unstoppable

UNSTOPPABLE

Marie Louise Irving

TIFFANY HOUSE
Australia

I received this message from Bishop Martin

"In my devotion this morning, God placed my heart's attention on the message you sent,"

We will run the race set before us and not be distracted from our end goal to eradicate world poverty.

"The more I pray about these words, the more the Lord affirms in my spirit that if we refuse to be distracted, but maintain a walk of faith and focus on Christ the author and finisher of this vision, we will see the Lord move across the world raising the lowly and the poor from the dungeon of oppression and affliction. We will be Christ's feet (walking in the streets and lives of the outcasts in society) and Christ's hands (embracing the most hurting with love). Then shall the light of the Lord shine among the nations, and the good news of the kingdom of God be proclaimed higher and further in the earth.

Be encouraged, Marie, you are championing a global vision that God is turning to be His banner and safety net for the weak, which is the cry of all the bible prophets and within the Law of Moses.

I find it such a privilege to work alongside such a servant of God as yourself Marie! Thanks for carrying the heart of God."

Bishop Martin

AND I GIVE UNTO YOU A NEW NAME

Revelations 2:17

STALWART
Standing firm in the face of adversity

UNSTOPPABLE
Moving forward in the face of adversity

CONTENTS

Part One

Foreword

I have had the honour of knowing Marie Irving for over twenty years and working alongside her in various local community programs for much of that time. *Unstoppable* is a thoroughly engaging record of Marie's own memories from the 80+ years of her inspirational life.

Unstoppable describes Marie Irving perfectly.

Despite many setbacks and challenges, she has remained faithful to God's calling and as a result, thousands of lives have been impacted and changed for the better. With the perfect mix of humility, vulnerability, and unshakeable faith, you are sure to be inspired by all that God has done and continues to do through this godly woman.

Perhaps the best commendation with which I can honour Marie is the confidence I have that her work will remain 'unstoppable' long after she goes home to be with her Lord, whom she's served so faithfully for just on sixty years.

My prayer is that as you read this book and hear how Marie has followed God's calling for her life, that you'll be inspired to find and follow God's calling for yours, be that across the street or throughout the world.

Pastor Rohan Bell
Lead C3 Pastor
Camden Picton Thirroul

PART ONE

The journey started when I was young

it was full of trouble and of fun

1938- 1945

1

WAR YEARS

With a juddering crash, the front door catapulted along the hallway, windows showering shards of glass everywhere. Mam yelled, "Quick girls, get to the kitchen table!" Under the heavy maroon, damask table cloth that reached the floor, my little sister and I crouched low. In our secret hideaway, we held each other tightly. Amid the bombings, every time, I was never afraid. It was a game for us.

Life was anything but ordinary – blackouts every night and air raid wardens patrolling the streets yelling, "get that blipping light off." Then the wailing sirens and the crashing and running as we fetched our Micky Mouse Gas Masks from the cardboard box. The danger was everywhere. During the night time bombings, my mam made it a game as we raced through the pitch black to the bomb shelter. Once back home, she'd brush off her fright and make a cup of tea.

My story begins watching my parents maneouver our family through some very dark days during wartime England in the 1940s. We lived in Blyth, Northumberland, near a submarine base frequently bombed during WWII. One warm sunny day, a visiting family friend and my sister and I were out walking. We came upon a beach, and I ran out towards the soft sand in the same typical fearless fashion, I would walk right smack into danger later in my life. Playing and gleefully skipping along the edge of the water seemed harmless enough until our friend shouted, "Get OFF the beach! Mines are everywhere!"

At home, Mam tried calming her shattered nerves with a fresh pot of tea. With her head in her hands, she quietly squealed, "Didn't you see that sign, Mrs. MacFarlane?

Danger. Mines. Do not enter? And how on earth did the girls get inside that fence? "

Even though nervy, and rightly so, mam loved people, and it appeared my sisters and I would be just like her. "There is always room at our house – the more, the better," She'd say as she opened the patched-up front door in response to the government's decree that workers from the submarine base squash in with us. Our first billets, a husband and wife, slept in the oversized front bedroom. Mam, Margot and I squashed together in the tiny back room, barely enough for a double bed and a wardrobe.

Those days were cruel. Yet, mam was determined to carry on unhindered by the chaotic war thundering around her. She was down to earth and practical, and to keep her mind off all the things that frightened her, organised a strict routine of daily chores. Mondays were washdays. Everyone in the street washed their laundry in tubs full of hot water and then strung them all out across the communal back lane. By midday, the lane was colourfully festooned from one end to the other. Equally, every Saturday evening, the hot water was carried into the living room for our weekly bath time and poured into a tin bath warmed by the open coal fire.

Being strict was only one side to mam. She also was a dreamer and, as such, was large as life. I saw this at a time when meat was scarce, and looking upon near-empty dinner plates at night, mam brought a pig home, and Margot and I named her Daisy. Of course, we didn't know of her plight, nor did she. Every morning, with our heavy buckets of slops, we'd walk about four blocks away to feed her. Yet on Christmas morning, Margot and I, distraught, searched everywhere. Mam was undecided between keeping a child's pet and putting Daisy on the Christmas table. "Oh, the girls will get over it," she mused.

But no, we didn't get over it. Instead, we wailed, "We can't eat Daisy." Mam was heartbroken at our sadness. Troubled, she gave all that meat away. That was nothing to sneeze at, for pork was pretty rare. In those war days, food was scarce, more so precious like a jewel and only gotten through coupons. Once I was caught red-handed eating a months' worth of sugar and was given a right smack for it. "All right, I'll never have sugar again," I pouted, and I never did from that day on. I remember pleading with my mother to have one of those delicious red things to eat, the elusive red ripe tomato that was the height of luxury to me. "But luxuries, my pet, are beyond us just now," she'd say.

While mam was a no-fuss person, dad always lived with his heart on his sleeve. Instead of finding food to eat, he was happily giving it away. When stationed in North Africa in the navy, he travelled from the war ravaged south England to us in the north. He was carrying with him a large stick of bananas to surprise us children. My father loved people too and was always striking up conversations. As the train rattled along, he would hear stories of the travellers' sick relatives. One by one, the bananas began disappearing. By the time he reached home, that stick was almost bare. So, while we didn't starve, we caught a glimpse of a father's heart that was soft and kind towards those suffering. We learned too, the finer things in life were luxuries, not necessities.

Scarlet fever

Margot and I were not quite two years apart and we shared a sisterly love for each other. Even amidst a raging war, we'd holiday at our favourite aunt's place. One balmy afternoon, Margot watched wide-eyed as I was suddenly rushed to an isolation hospital. The test showed Scarlet Fever. On a bed, the nurse wheeled me into a room, and there, for three months, I was on my own without a soul in the world to comfort me. As my body recovered, the sounds of an empty room became louder, and I felt abandoned.

When mam finally arrived, she held up some chocolate and stood helplessly behind a thick glass window. If mam wants to do something, she'll find a way to do it. So she cleverly slipped a thin bar of chocolate within the thick pages of a new book she had bought me. I eagerly opened it, but no chocolate in sight, probably stolen by a staff member! Then, on the day of discharge, my life took a sharp turn. The nurse came with devastating news, I had been in contact with a diptheria patient. "Another six weeks in isolation for you, little girl," she said. To a four-year-old, that door, now barred, and surrounding walls altered into a deeper and darker prison. *I'll never escape its coldness now,* I thought.

The summer of 1944 was particularly glorious. The long grinding war was in its fifth year. My mother, who hated sleeping outdoors but fed up with the war, decided to take us camping. At a place called Happy Valley, we had an exceptional holiday. I still have vivid memories running wild upon the moors and collecting cartridges from shallow streams up on the Northumberland heather-clad hills. It was indeed a happy place for me, mainly when mam bought us strawberry milkshakes from the milk bar. That first taste of creamy strawberries is still with me today, and seventy years later, I always visit that same milk bar when holidaying from Australia.

In May 1945, the war in Europe finally ended, and what a *slap-up* neighbourhood party we had. Of course, I had no idea the war had just ended. I thought the adults were celebrating us children as if to say, *aren't they the best*? The reward, paper coned lolly bags! The indescribable happiness was so tangible I could fill my hands up with it.

1946-56 school years

Not long after, I turned seven years old. Times were still pretty tough, and food rations continued for quite a few years afterward. Yet, the school holidays were full of long lazy sunny days. Without the threat of bombs, I loved playing outdoors and picnicking at the local beach with my family and a host of other kids. Often exhausted, we'd return home late into the afternoons.

It's around this time I'd see a challenge and say to myself, *'Yep, I can do that.'* The particular contest was to climb up the slide from the bottom at my favourite swing park. 'Easy as pie,' I'd say to myself. And up I scadalaled. Halfway up, I overbalanced, fell, and broke my arm. Cradling a wounded ego, I screamed as mam wheeled me into the doctor's surgery in a baby's pram. As the doctor tried to maneouver my excruciatingly painful arm out of my rare Fairisle jumper, mam pleaded, "Just cut the sleeve off," but no, he didn't. It never stopped me though. I would always be seeing a challenge and having a try, and I would continue pushing the envelope throughout my entire life.

I'd grown up with a love for books, theatre, and card-playing, and it all began at Aunt Margot's home. By now, at the ripe old age of seven, I had a strong belief in myself and was feeling very grown-up. Being the bigger sister, Margot and I travelled to her place on a big red double-decker bus with mam. Racing to the top deck, we plopped ourselves on the back seat and began singing lustily throughout the trip – much to everyones amusement.

While I enjoyed singing, even at that young age, I wanted to know everything there was to know. I was curious about every single thing. At my aunt's place, books opened up that world to me. In every nook and cranny bookcases overflowed – even the staircase landing had shelves crammed with books. Open any cupboard, and books upon books would fall out. I especially revelled losing myself in Enid Blyton's *Famous Five Adventures*.

My aunt not only was an avid book lover, she also belonged to the local Dramatic Society and encouraged us to put on drama plays for the local kids charging a ha'penny or a comic.

In already overcoming some significant obstacles, I began seeing myself as a winner. And it was at night I would imagine myself winning every game - even though at this point I was losing, hopelessly so. We slept in an oversized double bed with our cousins. Two heads up one end and two heads at the other. We claimed to be inveterate and experienced gamblers; the four of us spent many hours honing our card gaming skills. I remember my sister owing my cousin "millions of pounds," and often, by torchlight under the blankets, we'd continue the game, engrossed long into the night. The thrill of winning and bantering in harmless competition would become a big part of my adult life.

I was ably conquering a child's world. I thought to have a try at the sorts of things adults do. For weeks before my eighth birthday, I had been scouring the streets for cigarette butts. As soon as we were left alone in the front room, we gleefully lit up cigarettes and puffed merrily away. A combination of party food and illicit smoking ended in a wretched night of vomiting. But I had learned a lesson and cigarettes had no appeal while growing up.

Even so, I had this thing of conquering the world under control. Not long after that wretched night vomiting up my birthday party food, I had taken the responsibility upon myself for most of my problems, and I worked out how to solve them. I needed money to go the pictures, and I found two little girls on their way to the shops in a laneway. I stood over them and took their money and ran off shouting threats back at them. Hardly an angelic thing to do. Two hours later, an outraged lady came knocking on our door. Mam could not believe that I would do such a thing and made sure I received a severe punishment for this misdemeanor. But it didn't stop me, even though I had to figure better ways of solving my problems.

2

INSATIABLE DESIRE

With the war now over and no longer governed by gas masks or bombing raids, we could holiday at the famous Butlins Holiday Camp. We soaked in the carefree atmosphere, splashed in their crystal blue pools, and enjoyed the sheer luxury of abundant food. Margot and I spent hours playing in real storybook castles, pretending to be fairytale princesses. Everything was incredibly wonderful for us. Throughout my life, experiencing wonderful moments, holidaying in foreign places would continue to gladden my free spirited heart.

Weekends were exhilarating, zooming out past the houses and shops in our little van. As we neared the seaside, I'd breathe in the salt air and on the beach, hear magical sounds of waves toppling each other and sand squelching through my toes. Squinting into the distance, I'd look ahead for glistening treasure, just as my uncle taught me.

But it was my dad that gladdened my heart the most. He saw a lady walking along the dunes with a bunch of kids. After a brief chat, he discovered the kids were orphans. Overcome with compassion, my father reached into his pocket and put one pound into the lady's hand.

"Here, give the kids a treat at the café," he said. I felt proud of him.

My parents were a tremendous inspiration to me. I saw their zest for life, and I felt I could trailblaze behind them. With fresh memories of my father's big and generous heart, one Christmas, my sister Margot and I rugged ourselves up, walked out into the snow, and began knocking on the neighbour's doors. Door-to-door carolling was a common practice, with every child's high hopes of receiving a mince tart or some Christmas cake or, even better, a shilling. One year, we gathered a small fortune of six shillings and sixpence and decided to give it to the sick children in the local cottage hospital. The surprised matron suggested, "Why don't you buy some toys for the children?" So off we went happily to the shops and came back with our carefully chosen toys.

I then began dreaming about the sort of money I needed to give away and was offered a weekend job at my uncle's corner shop. It was just after my ninth birthday and he paid my wages in lollies- that suited both him and myself. Then he began seeing a tenacious nature in me, so he taught me how to chop kindling wood with his sharp axe. For that, extra lollies were put into my bag.

Then, in the warmer months, my mother took over the shop for a couple of hours in the afternoons, while he led a gaggle of kids to look for glistening treasure in the sand- something he'd rather do than earn money in a day's work at the shop.

But there were limits. I would rather stay in bed in the pre-dawn below zero temperatures during the bitter winter seasons, than to get up when delivering papers on my pushbike.

***

I had an insatiable desire to learn and took the idea of going to school very seriously. I was diligent, persistent more so, and soaked up everything seen and heard in the classroom. Arithmetic wasn't my top subject, nor my favourite, so I had to be smart in the way I handled this subject. My teacher was struggling to get his class successfully through the final exam. Instead of making the learning fun, he, with a leather strap, would angrily whack anyone who got the sums wrong. "That'll teach you to remember," he'd say.

I now had a new problem to solve, one of not getting that strap. Remember, I am only a kid. But a devious one! To trick him, I worked out which sums I ought to have got right and which ones it was okay to get wrong, and then I would blatantly lie. For, you see, my heart was set on going to Grammar School, and to get there, I needed to pass that final exam.

When the results came out, they were undecided about my entry for I had barely passed. But luckily, the news came with an invitation to meet with the principal. After the interview, there was an essay to write and a puzzle to do. I walked home in a flood of tears, distraught as there was no way I could trick them into thinking I knew what I was doing with that puzzle. After a tense time of waiting, a letter arrived informing me that I had been successful.

Oh, the relief and utter joy! My determination was rewarded and put me on a path of lifelong learning which ultimately would lead me along a track crammed with new opportunities.

I had barely settled into the school routine when my parents surprised me with the news of "a little sister on her way!" With the war four years behind me and loads of English, Latin, French, and history ahead, I knew a crying baby would hinder my studies. But the immediate bonus of welcoming our little sister Heather into the world was a holiday at Christmas time.

Because of possible birth complications, baby Heather needed to be born at a distant maternity hospital near Allendale, the village my dad had grown up in. My father's best friend invited us to stay through the New Year. Even though mam was in the hospital, Margot and I made the most of this little holiday. Some highlights were the personally inscribed iced biscuits from the bakery and the exciting time we had rugging up on freezing nights for the ancient New Year Eve festivals. The blizzard didn't stop the noisy fanfare and colourful street marches.

It was my grandfather, a fisherman, who taught me to adore the deep blue sea in all its many moods. Mam and Dad, too - after returning from the pub on very dark stormy nights, they'd get us up out from bed and dress us snugly and take us for a walk down to the harbour. It was sensational at the pier. The howling icy winds swept across my face, I'd brace myself with my gloved fingers wrapped around the railing, and cling tightly while pounding waves angrily lashed at my feet. The exhilaration of those nights has helped fuel my extreme love for daring adventure.

I pushed pretty hard on the envelopes that came my way. I had often been warned not to give baby Heather chewing gum. While out with her one day, I decided to see what would happen. At first, I watched with fascination, but that quickly turned to panic as she began swallowing it. Two fingers down her throat, and the chewing gum was out in an instant. A lucky escape for both of us!

Not long after, we moved into a large four-bedroom house at the posh end of town. Shortly after that move, my father set his business up as a commercial traveller selling toys and other goods in Scotland. He left mam with little money in a house full of strange noises, the type of noises one hears when alone at night. Mam hated being alone, and I knew she dreaded it. Fear is contagious, and usually, if it isn't one fear, it is another, and I could see it hampering her otherwise energetic personality. I absorbed her nervousness and felt helpless to help her deal with this enigma, especially when around cats.

Even though I felt the fear, I believed in myself - enough to manoeuvre through life with the notion I was old enough to take on the world. One day a lady from across the road came collecting for charity; mam did not have a penny in the house. Even so, I was sent to get money out of my money box. I knew what was going on, and aware of my actions, I took the pink coloured chest to the front door and, with confrontational honesty, said, "mam, I can't get anything out of this box." My mother was mortified. She hated that house and missed living in our original street close to her parents and nine brothers and sisters. Within two years, we moved back into a bigger place there and became part of that big happy family again.

Then, just like that, I was no longer a cute little girl. At fourteen, I was plain and plump, and I hated my father calling me "Venus on a rock bun." Being conscious of my weight, sure, I was aware of that. But I was also aware of a greater dilemma, for my curious nature was fast maturing, and I questioned everything. Mam knew I could see beyond what she saw, and in the tug-a-war between us, she identified me as having a defiant and domineering personality. But I saw our disputes through my point of view – one she needed to know about. After another significant dispute, mam scolded me with, "I remember that sugar incident when you were a little girl. Marie, you always were an obstinate child." A defiant attitude, a bother then, but precisely the very thing needed to pioneer a world-changing program later in life.

I had my own life and parties to go

Then a thought interrupted
All that flow.

The noise in my head

and the intrigue in my heart

got me searching for answers from the very start.

3

THE SEARCH

By the time I was fifteen, I was full of bounce and confidence. I was told a boy said of me, "I have just met a young girl with the most beautiful blue eyes I have ever seen." Perhaps it was my skyblue eyes, but whatever it was, boys and I became inseparable. But all that fun stopped when in my final exam, I got my worst mark ever. I had always wanted to be a teacher, but being a girl made it challenging to achieve a professional career in those days. In 1956, I left school and started my working life as a bank clerk. Seriously, I don't know what I was thinking. After all, arithmetic was not the best subject nor even held the slightest interest to me. Even so, I tried my best, and after a few months in my new job, I was sent off to Newcastle- on-Tyne to learn how to use the Burroughs Adding machine.

The best part of the learning experience was the beautiful elegant Georgian Street. The little class assembled in the tiny attic at the head office. It was there we had oodles of tea breaks with pretty teacups and chocolate biscuits. It was more of a celebration of sorts than anything else—long lunch breaks and more pretty teacups and special chocolate biscuits mid-afternoon. One day we were given the entire rest of the day off to see the visiting Queen Mother. Back at the local bank the following week, I still had no idea what I was doing with those adding machines. I caused a fair bit of chaos in the afternoons after work as we checked the ledgers for up to two extra hours to find the mistakes.

In frustration, I remembered back to the stylish interruptions in the attic and realised I had hardly learned a thing. After three months, the manager kindly said, "We have been thinking about your career Miss Graham, and we feel you would be happier at a smaller branch." I was transferred to a tiny country bank – not a machine in sight! It was so dull and boring. It was there I took an interest in things I enjoyed doing, such as buying bunches of pretty flowers and handing them to the elderly as I walked home from work.

Then, one autumn day, I was at the cinema buying an ice cream when suddenly a question began spinning around in my head. It was so new to me, and I wondered if it was me asking it.

I tried controlling the noise it was making in my head, but it kept demanding an answer. Who am I, and why am I here? I felt my mind expand like a balloon with every thought about life's meaning. The next day, finding the answer became a driving force in my life.

I didn't know the nature of the question, so I thought, *perhaps the answer would be found in becoming a social butterfly?* To explore that idea, I decided to attend a party with a friend, but she didn't turn up. So, 'out of the blue,' I decided to go to the local dance – a completely new experience. I was astounded – the boys were falling all over themselves to dance with me. *It must be my new jumper,* and I wore it for the next three weeks until someone commented about not having any other clothes.

Surprisingly, my sudden great power over men went straight to my head, and ultimately, I became a supreme manipulator. On Monday and Saturday, I set up my dates at the dance, often   going out with two or three different guys each week. I aimed to see how quickly I could get them to propose to me, then flatly refused them. My greatest triumph was receiving two marriage proposals on the same night. It was a game, and I had no thought for their feelings, but I knew this lifestyle could not answer my questions. After a couple of years, the ache was still there.

Still misunderstanding the nature of my search, I thought I'd look for answers in sacrificial service. After all, that's what I had been taught in Sunday school. Could I also earn my way into God's acceptance? I was going to give it a great try. I loved children so thought to find the answer by working in a children's home, a beautiful old mansion in the country, situated fifty kilometres from home. I worked six days a week from 6 am to 9 pm as an assistant housemother to a family of ten children. I was asked to make scrambled eggs for breakfast the first day there, but I had no idea how to do this. At the end of my first week, I was left to make a roast dinner while the children went to church. Everything went well until I tried making the gravy, which turned out black. With a flash of inspiration added to it milk, convinced it would lighten the colour only to watch horrified as it curdled – I was on a steep learning curve.

The cruel winters made washing sheets just that much harder. It was bad enough I had to trudge down to the washhouse in the backyard in the freezing weather with these urinated sheets. Worse was plunging them into the icy water. My hands became painfully cracked, and the stinging was excruciating. While tending painful hands, I was still feeling the throb in my empty heart.

Sometimes, I would go to church youth conferences with my friend, where we heard something about being born again. My friend and I laughed uproariously at that idea – how stupid! Even though I was sent to Sunday school, the subject of God was never mentioned at home. So, with no intentions of opening up my heart to a new spiritual rebirth, I would walk out of those meetings completely unchallenged. Even so, I began thinking that if I started reading my Bible, I would find the meaning of life and, with that, the reason why I was here. I was determined those answers be found. *There has to be something in this Bible that would answer my questions*, I would tell myself.

Every week on my one day off, I would take a fifty-kilometre bus trip home to see my parents. At dusk, as I set off down the lonely two-kilometre track to the bus stop, I'd become absorbed by the snow-laden trees in the winter months.

Beautiful feelings filled my soul, so much so I thought it would burst on those moonlit nights. Entranced by the beauty around me, I would think about life and its meaning.

Yet as I strolled along the dirt track, I had within my hand a pot of pepper. My mother, who was very nervous at best, had given it to me with strict instructions to throw it in the eyes of any person accosting me. My imagination was as big as hers, and she had me fearing weird sounds or monsters jutting from behind trees. I decided singing would help- for that's what made the time go fast on my way to Aunt Margot's all those years ago. So, I sang as loud as I could, hoping that someone from a local farm might come and investigate if I stopped suddenly.

After three long years of learning new skills and the self-sacrificing work at the orphanage, I could not feel good enough for the God I was reading about in the pages of the bible. I still felt unworthy of His love, and in that sense, was unable to do anything within my power to reach Him. The bible only made my search more impossible.

In desperation, I went to see the minister from the church where I had been a Sunday school teacher. Indeed, he would help me understand my torment. I told him I felt, after searching my bible, God demanded perfection. "What shall I do?" I wailed. "I can never be perfect, living up to this standard; it just seems too hard." He replied, "I think you should go and see a psychiatrist." I was devastated. If a minister thought this, I was in big trouble. *Am I going mad? Am I looking for something that doesn't exist?* In asking these questions, a thick cloud of unknowing fell over my life. Meaning and purpose disappeared, and I was surrounded by utter darkness.

By this time, I was terrified that my life would never find meaning. I did not like the sun going down, and I hated going to bed. I rarely slept well. Night after night, terrible black fears assailed me, and I felt I was sinking into a deep feeling of loss and even depression. No one was there to help me.

The meaning of life was beyond my reach. I had tried everything. I had tried pleasure. I had tried to be a good girl by leading a sacrificial life. I had tried reading my Bible. Nothing worked. I determined to have one last try. I would become a hard-core party-going girl. By this time, I was working at the blood transfusion service, and three of my workmates were moving down to London. To run away from my possessive boyfriend, I went with them.

Accommodation

My mother was concerned about accommodation. My cousin had a friend who might put us up, so I told Mam we were all organised. The friend was not at home when we arrived, and her reticent flatmate sent us away. It was 9.30 pm when we returned, hoping against all hope to find a bed. My cousin's friend was very welcoming and gave us the floor to sleep on. Here, I met for the first time Australians who seemed to be constantly coming and going. I was fascinated by their "She'll be right mate" attitude as they all piled in together, warmed by their sleeping bags on the floor. Their zest for adventure was contagious.

Within a week, we moved into the flat directly above us. It was the swinging sixties in London, and jobs were easy to come by. I began looking for work, and by the end of the first day, I had three positions from which to choose. I started as a receptionist at Colgate Palmolive. I loved the buzz of London, and all of our money was spent on new clothes.

Food was a very low priority, and we only ate well if we were taken out for dinner by some boyfriend. Our weekly treat each Friday night was a Mars Bar, divided into four and eaten very slowly. The other girls went wild. There were boys everywhere, and within a short time, one of the girls was pregnant. I was on my way to joining them in their riotous living.

I had a double life and was two-timing myself. On the surface, I appeared easy-going, yet deep down, I was still desperately unhappy, suffering from deep fears and contemplating suicide. Nothing at all satisfied. At my point of utter despair, my dear friend Shirley, who had become a Christian since I last saw her, invited me to church. I had tried so many churches and found nothing there, so no, I was not interested. *Definitely not*!

However, I did not want to be rude, so I said, "yes," out of politeness. As the Minister began to preach, it was as if he was speaking only to me. He told me that Jesus had died for me and had taken my sins upon Himself on the Cross, and a tremendous burden lifted from me. *That's what I have been looking for all of these years*. Oh, the joy!

After almost six years of searching, I eventually heard the gospel and found the Truth. Life now had meaning, and my heart was overjoyed. That night I was converted at Westminster Chapel under Dr. Martyn Lloyd Jones, one of the foremost preachers in England. My Christian journey had begun.

Follow me upwards, be careful to go

only on the path

I will show.

4

THE DINNER

The girls I had moved to London with were getting out of hand. To help me survive the transition, Shirley invited me to join the Antioch, a supportive Christian group organised by Derek Elphinstone, an actor as large as life itself. His charismatic nature made faith in Jesus relevant and he attracted many from the media and the arts culture. Then Joan and Rod, recent newlyweds, offered me a room with them until I found a suitable place.

Over the next six months, my early Christian life was a struggle. One weekend I was left in their flat on my own, and I became overwhelmed with memories of being alone in a big house when dad was away. I was conditioned to think it was unsafe. My imagination then found ways to connect the fear to something that I could not control. The only thing that made me feel vulnerable were the two old ladies on the top unit, whom I had never met. They might have been some soul's kind and gentle greataunts for all I knew. But illogically, I had myself convinced they would flip out and kill me with an axe.

I felt unable to protect myself. Eventually, at four o'clock in the morning, a boy from Antioch had to come to keep me company. As he sat with me, obviously praying quietly, his persona, and the peace filling the room was incredibly calming. Alongside trying to manage mam's fears, I was still suffering a dreadful sense of dark emptiness, symbolising something of a dark night, where my soul could not find its way forward. I had found salvation for my spirit, but I had still not overcome the fears that overwhelmed me as a child.

I could keep myself busy during the day, but at night,

foreboding darkness wrapped itself around my mind. Call it a monster, a mocker, but whatever it was, I could feel it but not see it. Battling this intense enigma was incredibly tiring. I was determined to get this ridiculing scorn gone for good and surprisingly found verses in the Bible that seemed to have an invisible power. I was helped immensely from chapter 10 in Corinthians, from which I came to understand that God would not allow anything I could not handle to overpower me. Instead, He would give me strategies to overcome it.

And I did overcome it with the sound of my voice. Reciting those Scriptures prised the darkness off my mind. In this sense, God's Word drew a boundary line around my life - enough was enough. During times of intense stress, I trained myself to believe God's Word and as I did, a bright light of hope shone into my heart, and the meaninglessness of life slowly, but indeed surely, began disappearing. Eventually, after six months, those Scriptures became a ray of warm sunshine, thawing off the ice after a long hard winter. It indeed was an assuring comfort that I would not experience anything darker than I could cope with. The cold, horrific darkness never returned. The fear was conquered forever!

The tremendous support of both Scripture and my friends from Antioch enabled me to survive the ordeal. I had learned to use God's word. Yet, I was still very much focused on myself - true freedom would only be mine as I got my eyes off myself.

Dorothy from Northumberland and her friend Sylvia and I moved into a tiny attic flat. Having always been fascinated by history, I joined the local night classes. Most weekends, the class visited historic sites and often finished up at a pub of ancient interest. I continued loving my new life in London with my Christian friends from Antioch. I mainly spent a lot of time with Shirley, who first invited me to church. She was from British Guiana, and many of her friends were from the Caribbean. At her parties, I was the only white girl, but I loved that. Her friends were so vibrant and full of life. Peter, her husband, had a little Morgan sports car, and I spent many happy hours sitting in the dicky seat at the back as we sped around London.

1963

New experiences every day! Lying in bed one Saturday morning, I heard the clip-clop of hooves as a troop of Horse Guards rode by. On another occasion, a bowler-hatted gent came speeding towards me on roller skates, *only in London,* I thought. It was this sheer unpredictability of everything that was so appealing and made me so very happy.

But God can also be unpredictable. Out of nowhere, I felt He was telling me to go back to Northumberland to share the gospel with my family. I was utterly devastated, and clearly, everything in me protested. But I could not escape His gentle pressure. So reluctantly, I handed in my notice at work, said goodbye to my Christian friends, and climbed aboard the Northumberland bound train.

My family thought that I had become a religious fanatic. I took my sister Margot to church. She was horrified, and at the end of the service, she turned to me and very scathingly said, "No way, Marie, forget it, I'm not interested full stop." Heather, my other sister, was equally unimpressed and would complain when I read my Bible.

My Aunt Margot, who had always been my favourite and whom I loved dearly, became very ill and was dying from cancer. She was only fifty-four. I had watched her go to church and give every child a Bible for their twenty-first birthday. I knew she was a Christian; she believed Jesus died for her sins and had given her a new heart. Yet I felt God tell me to write and share the hope of heaven, and therefore there is no fear in dying. Yet, in my early days as a new Christian, I thought it was presumptuous of me to be encouraging her about certainties of the salvation of her soul. I hesitated for many weeks but eventually sent the letter which she received while in hospital. A few days before she died, she had a vision of heaven and kept saying, "But oh, it was so wonderful." There was no fear of dying.

1964

Dorothy came to Northumberland to visit her sister and invited me to their house for dinner. For many months she had been trying to get me to meet a childhood friend of hers. "Douglas is the life and soul of any party," She'd tell me. "You would really like him." Of course, it's the way fairy-tale lovers meet, but I intentionally went out of my way to avoid meeting him; he sounded a pain in the neck. Of course, she purposely forgot to tell me there'd be a surprise waiting for me at dinner. When I arrived, he was there also.

Doug was exciting and very attractive. Despite my prejudice, he was charming and witty, and more importantly, he had just returned from the Mediterranean and the Middle East installing Radar Stations. I was impressed that he had worked there. That night he was reminiscing about a situation at the top of a high mountain in Turkey. Someone said, "Dougie, move that four-wheel drive." Even though he couldn't drive, he obligingly hopped in and clumsily put the car into reverse, sending the back wheels over the precipice. A quick-thinking Turkish soldier flung himself onto the bonnet to stabilise the vehicle, and Doug fled the car. His stories were highly fascinating, and jokes were funny, and I had a wonderful time enjoying his sense of sophistication. I also noticed his eyes-catching mine over the dinner table.

Doug's parents were emigrating to Australia, and they wanted Doug to join them. Dorothy was down in the dumps one day, and Douglas, to cheer her up, said, "Well, how about coming to Australia with me." She said yes. Dorothy was in and invited me to come along. One afternoon, she asked Douglas to take some pamphlets over to me. That's how we started dating.

On our first date, Doug arrived two hours late. For anyone

else, I would have been furious, but this guy was different. We stopped off at a pretty spot overlooking a tiny island known as Charlie's Garden; there, unexpectedly, he kissed me. My heart was smitten. From that captivating moment, we drove to an exotic Greek restaurant where we talked for hours. At 2 am he finally took me home. Just as I was about to get out of the car, he gently pulled my arm close to him and said, "Hey, why don't we go and see the sunrise." Doug found a very romantic spot near a ruined Priory overlooking the sea. From there, we walked down the cliff steps to the cold sand on the beach and saw the prettiest clouds form as the sun rose. Doug was the epitome of adventure, and I sensed I wanted to share it all with him.

Our relationship was becoming serious, and I knew it, so I invited Doug around to meet my parents. I suspected he'd be in his typical unconventional mood, but I had no idea that instead of walking though the open gate, he'd jump over the flower box atop the low brick wall. On hearing the crash, I came running out to find him sprawled all over the lawn and the flower box smashed.

Inside my house, sporting an old pair of tweed trousers with a hole in the knee, he graciously brushed himself off and greeted my parents. The following day, my mother was not amused and said, "Why are you going out with this man? I am more impressed with your current boyfriend."

Doug didn't look the part to her, but I was looking for something more than the other fellas had. In Doug, I found it. I was after the heart.

You must listen carefully,

so you don't lose your way.

Read lots
and listen to what they say.

5

TEN POUND POM

Everything about Doug was enormously wonderful and striking, and tumbling head over heels with my darling was very easy. Yet, he was not a Christian, and in my mind, I was playing with fire. After three months of falling deeply in love, I made a tough decision. As hard as that was, I drastically decided to finish the relationship. The next day, unaware of my intentions, he asked to go to the bible shop. "I'd like to understand more about God," he said. I was relieved as I so wanted him to enter into an adventure with his creator. He happily bought a Bible- a great confirmation that God had his hand on us—another three months passed with our feelings for each other growing stronger. Yet while he read his Bible, he hadn't surrendered his life to Jesus. In despair, I decided to finish the relationship. Again, not realising my intentions, he said, "I wish you'd pray for me- I want to believe, but something is stopping me." He did not have to wait long, for shortly afterward, we travelled down to London for the weekend.

On Sunday morning, we attended my old church, Westminster Chapel. In the afternoon, Doug spent time with some guys who witnessed to him, while my friends and I prayed for him. At the evening service, Doug was a completely different person, and he had given his heart to Jesus. Praise God! I was so happy. Doug became well acquainted with God's word and enjoyed sharing it with strangers, and always prayed on his knees.

Doug's zest for life and passion for adventure was a strong pull on my heart. Yet, despite my deep love for him, I could see I was standing in my own way of marrying him. Even though I wanted to trek with him in the most incredible adventure, I continued to make plans with Dorothy, my lovely Christian friend. Within a few weeks, we were offered passage to Australia, so we became ten-pound Poms. I said goodbye to Doug. How could I stand by and let him go just like that? If I looked deep enough, I could see him following me out, and somehow, I knew it would be his journey with God. By this time, Doug was endearing himself to my parents, who invited him to stay with them after I left.

There was oodles of spare time on the boat, and to fill in some of it, I read about a man who lived in stark contrast to all I had grown up with. On every other page, I would read sentiments stating your life is found by serving others and giving it away to God. Every day, Hudson Taylor was my companion, and his journals were readjusting my focus. Dorothy thought I had turned into a nun.

While the journals were filling that previous deep emptiness, at night, the fun-filled memories of the world of pleasure I'd grown up in lay deep within my mind, and this made my trip particularly exciting. We met up with some young people and had a ball.

The ship sailed through the Suez Canal, and I decided to get off at Cairo, hoping to visit the pyramids at Giza and the Cairo Museum and re-join it a couple of days later at the other end of the Red Sea. In Cairo, I stayed at the Nile Hilton with an Australian girl. In the evening, we went clubbing with some pilots from Pan American Airway that we had met. I was quite a good dancer, and after doing the twist on the dance floor, my partner and I got a standing ovation. Next up was a belly dancer, but I could see she was furious with me for stealing her thunder. Every time she danced past our table, she would lean over and pull my long blonde hair. I was pushing the limits once again. So, as well as making sure I was ready for marriage, I still had a long way to go in my Christian commitment.

When the boat docked in Melbourne, a reporter from *The Age,* came on board looking for a story. News must have been slow that day because he took my picture playing deck quoits with the heading "Fun-loving Marie Louise, a social worker arrives in Australia." I told him I was a social worker expecting to do this because it had been my lifelong dream to help underprivileged people.

As the sun began rising on December 14, 1964, the boat sailed into one of the prettiest harbours in the world. I gasped at the beautiful views in Sydney, and Dorothy and I ran from one side of the ship to the other in order not to miss a single thing.

My cousin was supposed to meet the boat and all day we waited for her. I walked up and down the pavements, parading around Circular Quay displaying my name on a handwritten placard. At dusk, we received a message saying she had been delayed and, "I am attaching contact details for a place in Cremorne with Miss Straughan." She was eighty-eight years old and had never married. All her life, she had lived with her sister, who had recently died. She hated men and was a tough person to please.

Dorothy and I had $60.00 between us. The first week Dorothy spent all her money on new clothes. No one was hiring, and everything was shut down as it was the Christmas holidays. That didn't stop my work search, and on the 2nd of January, I started as a receptionist for the Australian Museum. I loved the people and the job, and catching the ferry to the city every day was my idea of heaven. However, Dorothy couldn't find a job, and for the first three months, we lived on one wage. Eventually, we bought a typewriter in a pawn shop, and I taught her to type. She then found work.

In our modern individualist age, focusing on ourselves is common, but more so typical. In Hudson Taylor's Journals, I was being gripped by a soul who didn't live his life for himself but breathed his breath for others. I was resolute to the same idea.

One day, circulars advertising the need for volunteers at the upcoming Royal Easter Show were put on my desk. *Hmm, looks fascinating,* I thought. So, willingly I put my name down and was rostered one shift at the Department of Education stall. That day I was enthusiastic to be offering my time and talent. Yet people kept looking at me with question marks all over their faces. I had been in Australia a mere few months, and trying to inform people about something of which I knew nothing was embarrassing! Even so, it ignited a lifetime love for the Easter Show and throwing off the bad experience; I began a life of volunteering and, with it, a passion for helping others.

Meanwhile, Miss Straughan, well, it wasn't easy to please her. One Sunday afternoon, we came home from the zoo with our boyfriends to find our bags sitting on the porch. I knew our relationship had deteriorated, but not that much to be evicted! After a frantic search, we moved into a ground-level flat in Leichhardt.

I soon learned all those creatures I had read about in books by Australian authors were not imaginary after all, but true. The first night there, I snuggled up in bed and opened my book to read. In the night's quietness, to my horror, I saw a dreadful creature scurrying across the floor. The more I looked, the more they appeared and the more terrified I became. On hearing a scream, Dorothy came running into my room, but she had taken her contact lenses out and couldn't see anything. "It's all in your imagination," she said. I ran out of the room and refused to go back and sleep there. So, Dorothy and I had to share the double bed in her room. Every night I'd come home from work in tears at the thought of scrubbing out the kitchen drawers and bombing the house. Nothing seemed to work.

I was home alone one evening, and in bed, I plumped up the pillow. To my horror, a cockroach ran out of the pillowcase. Hysterically I jumped up, screaming, and ran out of the front door, which promptly banged behind me. There I was outside in my nightie. Two teenage boys upstairs heard me screaming, climbed in through my bathroom window, and opened my front door, much to my relief. Oh, how I longed to be back home in England, but I was living from hand to mouth. I would just have to tough it out and cope with the unbearable cockroaches. I made the commitment to be here in Australia, so I determined to continue on and rough it out.

It was just as well, as mail from Douglas informed me that he was tramping his way overland towards "his love," as he called me. I read how he had sold his beloved white VW beetle to finance the trip, and in the dead of winter, through January's freezing snow, he began walking towards a girl who had warmed his heart. As the letters kept coming, I read how he only accepted rides when offered and never hitched. His first lift was with a man whose car was full of guns and, in Doug's words, "had more armour than a battleship." He insisted on the cartridges being emptied.

Then, his path of faith got a bit steeper later when he slept on an open fish slab in Italy and in Turkey, praying fervently when growling wolves surrounded his tent. Later, while crossing that beautiful country, he was walking along a very lonely road when a driver stuck his head out the window and yelled, "Hey Dougie, what are you doing here?" Recognising his old work colleague, he happily jumped in.

In these letters, I could see how he loved the variety of cultures and seemed to revel in every interaction, fascinated with the tiniest of worries and fancies in people's lives. He had a keen eye for detail. One time walking from Athens along a winding road, he stopped for a coffee and wrote in his diary, "I talked with the owner's grandson who showed me his books which were amply illustrated and beautifully presented. His grandmother refused payment for the coffee and instead told me about her bitter recollections of the war."

Much later, with three months of mail piled on my dressing table, I began thinking it would take him five years to reach me. That devastating thought added to the difficult period I was having adjusting to my new country.

Rather than the years, it only took five months to finally arrive in Pakistan, where he caught a boat to Sri Lanka to pick up the P&O cruiser to Australia. By this time, he had, with the last bit of his money, bought a watermelon which was to last him for his three-day journey down the coast of India. He shared some space in the ship's hold with the Indians who were cooking curries and chapattis.

Not long after leaving the shoreline, the automatic steering failed. From Doug's papers, the captain noted his knowledge in electronics, so he was sought out. Douglas hardly looked like a respectable engineer. Instead, he looked more like a hobo after five months on the road, sporting an unkempt bushy beard and a ragged shirt. After explaining the problem, the captain asked for Douglas's help. Even though Doug knew nothing about automatic steering, within minutes, he spotted a blown fuse. He checked all the equipment and finally replaced the blown fuse, and hey presto, the automatic steering restarted. Needless to say, the captain was delighted. "First class cabin and first-class food," he enthused. "But you're not coming into the first-class dining room looking like that!" God provided for him in his time of need.

On the 7th of May, 1965, I slipped on my new dress, and with a heart full of joy, I walked down George Street towards Circular Quay. The crisp morning air matched my brisk steps, and my heart sang, bursting with knowing. The long wait had finally ended. At my first glimpse of Doug, I ran into his arms and felt deeply held by his strong embrace. Douglas reached into his shirt pocket and pulled out a torn and tattered card with a beautiful rose on it. I opened to "je t'aime," "ti amo," "seni seviyorum," and *I love you* in Farsi, Punjabi, and Greek. He was passionate but penniless.

Awash with emotion, he bought a penny stick of liquorice that came with a ring- which he took from the packet and slipped on my finger!

Within a couple of days, Doug started work with AWA, and after dithering on my part for so long, we set the wedding date for six weeks later, 26th June. In the meantime, we found a church in Kingsford, where shortly afterward, Doug was baptised. The next six weeks passed in a whirl of activity. We did, however, find time to spend a weekend camping. We caught the train to the end of the line and hiked down to a lonely beach, and pitched the tent in the dark. We woke to the sun blazing in on us and imprint of feet, and the sound of hundreds of early morning swimmers. To our horror, we were, in fact, at one of Sydney's most popular beaches.

My lover, I married, and a family
we grew| started a career, a
work-life anew.

6

A NEW LIFE

Organising a wedding within six weeks and paying for it with the little money we had, was no easy task. Doug was still wearing his worn-out boots - in fact, everywhere he went, they were on his feet. With nothing that looked anything like new, in desperation, we prayed to God. The next day my cousin rang. "I've got some kitchen items. Are you interested?" she asked. We had absolutely nothing to start married life with, so Doug and I dashed across to her place. On top of the kitchen pile was a pair of brand-new black shoes, Doug's size! What rejoicing we had that night. However, two days before the wedding, we still did not have the best man, even with much prayer. At 9.30 pm that evening, we answered a knock at the door. There stood a new friend from church with some books. "Come in," we said enthusiastically to Colin. "You're our answer to prayer!"

I arrived at our Kingsford church in a white VW beetle owned by a friend and resplendent in a wedding dress and borrowed veil. There, after promising our love to each other, Douglas slipped on a gold band, inscribed "His love, our love, one love." Dorothy's Dutch boyfriend organised the photographer as a wedding gift, and a boy from work booked a cottage at Pearl Beach (now a millionaire's enclave). We had a blissful weeklong honeymoon for the princely sum of $20. All our wedding needs were miraculously supplied, and we learned the eternal truth, "My God shall supply all your need, according to his riches in glory by Christ Jesus." Phillipians 4:19 NKJ

We happily commenced married life in a brand new tiny bedsit in Surry Hills. Within a couple of months, I began to feel sick – yes, you guessed it, I was pregnant. Not what we had planned, but we were just so thrilled.

Doug had walked across parts of Europe and some of the Middle East to marry me and his love for walking never waned. One weekend, the delightful walk between Surry Hills and Vaucluse House, filled with scented wisteria, gladdened our romantic hearts. It also inspired possibilities in us as we strolled past the architectural beauty of the super-rich homes.

The bedsit suddenly became too small for our growing family, so we moved across the road to a larger old terrace house. There, we became house group leaders to an Antioch group. Doug was passionate about God and everything related to his faith. He took God's word seriously and was incredibly respectful, often kneeling in prayer, which was just not done in those days.

God had accepted him, and now, others deserved to know He accepts them as well. Douglas met Ray, a young man whom he barely knew, yet often spoke for hours with him about the redemption of mankind. Shortly afterwards, we received the shocking news that he had died from leukemia. He was unaware of his illness, but Ray accepted Jesus to be his Lord, so we rejoiced in the knowledge that he had gone to heaven.

I was still finding it horribly tricky adjusting to household vermin, for in England, there are no cockroaches, snakes, or venomous spiders as such. I resigned from work, and to help with the finances, six weeks before our little son was born, we took in a lodger. On her first night, she asked Douglas to unbolt two small windows, which he happily did. An hour later, horrified, she came racing upstairs, for two huge, oversized rats were running all over the walls in her lounge room. I was aghast watching Douglas frantically chase them with a broom. Eventually, an hour later, he shut the door and with nowhere to go, they fled out the window, which Douglas then hurriedly rebolted.

It might have been all that excitement, but suddenly I

was bent over with gripping pains. I thought a plate of all bran would fix me as it had usually done in the past with constipation. But after a few mouthfuls, the pains intensified, and then it dawned on me. I screamed out to Douglas, "Call a taxi." We rushed to the hospital, and within two hours, Graham was born.

All of my maternal support was on the other side of the world, so I decided to go to the Tresillian home in Nielsen Park. In that luxurious home, once owned by the famous Wentworth family, I was taught how to care for our little son. In the mirrored walled dining room, I ate delicious food and then relaxed in a pretty garden that followed a path down to the harbour. After being wonderfully nurtured and receiving instructions, I felt thoroughly confident to be the mother I dreamt of becoming.

In those early days, I saw God's protection, especially when Graham was four months old. He was sleeping quietly in his bedroom when I heard a tremendous bang. Racing upstairs, I found that a large part of the plaster ceiling in his room had crashed inches from his cot. Completely unharmed, Graham slept peacefully. When life has a way of *crashing around us,* I have learned that there is a place of protection in God's arms. We thanked God for his defence of our baby boy.

We moved from Surry Hills to Woolloomooloo. Life was tough, for we were living on one wage and saving for a house. There wasn't much money- I remember walking two miles to save two cents on a can of evaporated milk and haunting the fruit shops in the late afternoon for bruised fruit and vegetables. Yet, at a time before take-away, as a special treat, on Friday nights at Little Italy's restaurants the waiters filled our plates up with spaghetti bolognese, and we ate at home. God gave me the spaghetti to look forward to, so it softened the blow in times of scarcity.

Doug was making a lot of new adjustments, especially

to our new church. He was desperately missing his tight-knit Christian friends in England. Back there, Antioch was budding and blossoming. Here, a bitter winter had set in. Music was not allowed and metrical psalms were only sung after a tuning fork twanged a particular note .... Joy was as absent as the sun on a bitter cold wintery day, and it was enough to drain every bit of faith from us.

Doug had within him a beautiful pastor's heart. He tried getting everyone enthused in a small midweek group we were both leading. "Some members of the group are very worldly; they are no different to anyone else," he'd bemoan afterward.

Doug could not understand how, in the presence of a warm, tender-hearted *exuberant* God, people could look so cold, so dismal, and so, so bored. Worse, that they could be more interested in the world! In his mind, you were all in or all out. "I'll stop going to church for six weeks to sort myself out." A fateful decision.

Douglas was faced with another gigantic hurdle. He was skilled in engineering- perhaps overly so, yet formally he was unqualified. In England, with the scant bit of education he had during the war, he worked his way up into becoming a research and development engineer. Quite a feat.

One day he sat down at the kitchen table and said, "Any sixteen-year-old can do my job. I am working way below my capabilities and I feel dissatisfied. They say I need a formal university degree." We both knew he had the brains, so we prayed about it. Almost immediately, a job in the laboratories at the School of Electrical Engineering at one of the universities came up. Scant education or not, he had the willingness to push the envelope. His job application was successful. He then enrolled as a university student and began his formal education, cumulating in a doctorate in engineering.

While Doug was adjusting to his new direction, I fine-tuned

our routine at home to suit his schedule and our busy household. A lot was going on in our full house. We had just brought our second son Mark home from hospital and there was much rejoicing at his birth. Dorothy's sister and her family had emigrated from England and had come to stay with us. Then, thanks to a wedding gift from my parents, we had just brought a new home in Hillsdale.

After our visitors left, I was at home alone. Day in and day out, unable to get out much, I was feeling deserted. Doug was busy at work and didn't arrive home until late evening. Although still praying together, our spiritual path was distinctly going downhill. I struggled to believe God was, in fact, with me. My faith in His goodness was dwindling. So much so, it seemed I had fallen into a deep hole. To prevent a loss of grip while clawing myself out, I held tightly onto everything I believed to be true.

As a young adult, it was my faith that willed me back to life, and if I gave up now, I would be totally destroyed. Something important was missing in my Christian walk, but I didn't know what it was. I tried re-dedicating my life at a Billy Graham crusade, but no, that was not it.

Catching my breath on a busy day over a cup of tea, I was watching a television program about a Pentecostal church. I had never heard of such a church before, but noticed they had an infectious joy – a joy even that seemed desperately missing in my life. I needed to find out more. In the phone book, the nearest Pentecostal church was miles from where we lived. With two small children and no car, I thought it was out of the question for me to go there. So, I prayed, "If that is what I need God, you've got to show me." Even without the answer, I began feeling a sense of hope filling my soul.

It was the beginning of the charismatic renewal in the early 1970s, and within a few days, God led me to a handful of people in my church who had opened their hearts to receive the peace and power of the Holy Spirit. Using his minibus, a gentleman took me and others to various meetings. I was appalled. Hands raised in the air, and the clapping all seemed so undignified. Strict protocol to church behaviour had gone out the window and I hated this sheer abandonment of propriety. It certainly was opposite to what I was used to.

Even so, the beautiful prophetic words were pulling me in, and I knew those words were God speaking and had come from heaven. Eventually, after three months, I decided that the question was not whether I liked it or not, but is it from God. If it is, then I hadn't any right to say I don't like it. I attended a Catholic church that had an after-service meeting for those wanting to have their hearts filled with joy.

So, one night shortly afterward, I decided I would stay back to be prayed for. During the main meeting that night, a man started to pray such a beautiful prayer that I felt drawn into its beauty. I raised my hands towards heaven, and I felt a heavenly language emerging from deep within me. And just like that, I was transported into a world full of warm emotions where I could actually feel what God feels - love and His peace and joy. I was hungry for more of God's peace and joy and of the power— the sort of feelings I felt when praying. The more I prayed, the hungrier I became. I wanted more of everything God had for me.

The training began, unknown then
the heart of
God,
I would defend.

The lonely, the lost, the poor in a land.

Forgotten by many but held by His hand.

.

7

DRIVEN WITHIN

I attended many meetings and became friends with those who also wanted more of God. One evening, an overseas visitor was facing a difficult situation and asked us to pray for God's wisdom. I was given a brief outline of this situation. I then began listening for God to speak to me. Moments later, I heard an inner voice say, "Go in faith, the Lord your God has sent you." I westled with the thought. I did not know his problem, so how could I be sure that I heard from God. The meeting closed and we stayed for coffee and cake. Somehow that coffee made a difference, and I got enough courage to approach the man. "These words have been going round in my mind all evening, 'Go in faith, the Lord God has sent you.' Does this mean anything to you?" I asked. The man looked at me in utter surprise and said, "Why yes! That's exactly what I needed to hear." So that night was the beginning of a flourishing prophetic ministry that has blessed me and others over the past fifty years.

When our little family moved to Carss Park, Doug was frantically achieving his doctorate, and I began attending the Christian Growth Centre. There at Sutherland, the new pastor John Wilkerson led us wonderfully into the deep things of God.

More than a belief, God was becoming a very dear friend. He spoke to me as any person would and conveyed messages using everyday situations. Once I had a picture of Jesus knocking on the door of my heart. In this picture, I saw myself opening the door and inviting Him in, expecting Him only to stay a short while. He said to me, "I do not want to be merely a visitor; I want to be free to come and go and not have to seek permission all of the time. I do not want you to have any rooms in which I am not welcome.

No secrets hidden away from me." I knew Jesus wanted to take up permanent residence in my heart and not be just an occasional visitor. As Jesus ever so gently began speaking to me, I could see He was *for* me and not against me. He was in my life for the long haul, and this empowered me and gave me inner strength.

It was within my mind these pictures were seen. One time I was praying when I saw myself sweeping a room. I heard a knock at the door and quickly swept all the dirt under the carpet. I then answered. It was Jesus. He strode right up to the place where I had hidden the dirt and bent down and turned back the carpet. In the light of his presence, there it was—all my dirt for Him and me to see. I felt so ashamed, but as the light emanated from Him, it began shrivelling up and disappeared. "Even in your sin, I love you. Don't hide your sins from Me," Jesus gently said. "Bring them to Me, and I will deal with them." God's warmth and goodness towards me was a magnetic force, drawing me in and creating a beautiful relationship between us.

Another time, I could see myself walking along a beach. Up ahead, I saw huge rocks preventing me going further. Ready to turn around and about to give up, suddenly, deep within my heart, I could hear God's gentle voice. "If you listen to my directions, you'll be able to scramble from rock to rock in certain positions, and you'll find a way through." This helped me understand how to get down and humble myself when faced with impossible problems in life. I began viewing God as a wise father who knew me well, One who keeps our issues private, never exposing our weaknesses. Instead, hidden from those close to us, He draws us in so that He can do surgery on our hearts.

He and I both knew that underneath my apparently "confident, focused and determined" posture was a very 'not so confident' girl. One Sunday, for instance, I had come into church quite late and sat in the back row. I loved my pastor with his deep voice and fiery passion and knew my quiet voice would never reach him if I had a word from this far back in the church. As I sat down, I prayed, "Please God, do not give me a word for those at the front will never hear me." But lo and behold, I had barely sat down when words did come into my mind very clearly. So, I spoke them out. As I began speaking, Ps John began to talk over me. Fearing I had done something wrong, my little hesitant heart became scared, and I went hot and cold. Yet a man and his wife, sitting just in front of me, listened to every word I spoke and, after the service, said, "That word was for our friends who came to church with us today, and they knew it." I had many misgivings about myself and later learned my voice was not even heard at the front. Jesus gently led me to depend on Him for the strength I needed.

Around this time, I worked as a secretary in the social work department of the local hospital. Assisting those who came with their queries was a joy, yet, I felt I had been created for something more challenging.

One day I overheard a conversation about a new TAFE welfare course, and I pricked up my ears. Afterward, I also spoke with the social worker about it and, with great anticipation, applied. In that first evening class, my heart soared with happiness. I was sure this new career path was God's plan for me. However, six weeks later, I was rather shocked to find myself pregnant again. Towards the end of the first year, I went into labour, and two days after our precious little son Frazer was born, I completed the final exam for the year while still in the hospital.

Douglas and I were slowly drifting apart. I wanted more of God, and he was not interested. Sometimes I would go to him with a problem, and he would say, "You've got a God, haven't you? Go to Him with your problems, not me." It was very hard, but it taught me an invaluable lesson to rely solely on God and not on anyone else. For the next two years, I had no separate income of my own. I was only allowed to tithe the housekeeping money, so I had little to give. The church was extending its property and made an appeal for finances for the building fund. I was in an impossible situation because I wanted to give but had no income. I prayed about it and asked God for some money of my own. Within a short time, I received a letter from England to say that my uncle Abie had died and had left me a small legacy. What a great God we have! I was able to give it to the building fund.

The famous Christian author Isabel Kuhn's riveting tales constantly stirred my spirit. For many years I had wanted to visit where she worked as a missionary in China. And many times, I asked Douglas to come with me.

"No, I am not interested," he said.

"Okay, if you do not want to go," I replied, "I will catch a train from Hong Kong into China when next returning from England." Doug was happy about that.

After work one afternoon, Doug dropped his bag on the couch and, after getting a cold drink from the fridge said, "You'll never guess what's happened today. I've been invited to go to China. There is a conference at the very place you wanted to go and the same week you were planning on going." I smiled. Life has a way of turning the tables in one's favour, and I thought to myself, *what an amazing answer to prayer!*

China was just now opening up after the cultural revolution, and it was wonderful to be visiting this beautiful country. After the conference, Doug and I planned some sightseeing. We missed our flight to an area of China we wanted to explore. The next flight was later that afternoon, and we had no where to go at the airport. There were no shops, simply nothing to see. "Can we go anywhere?' we asked the booking clerk. "Yes, of course, you can," he answered. Doug said, "Let's go and look at the airstrip." Moments later, two roaring jets swooped low and began to strafe the runway with their bullets. "There must be an Air Force base close by," Doug breathlessly said. Finally, after reaching our destination, we caught a bus to a famous temple site. The Taiwanese couple sitting in front of us were very friendly. After a long chat, the young woman invited us to where they were staying for a meal. That evening we walked into a house full of push bikes. To make room for us, they promptly wheeled them outside and erected the table. I noticed a platter full of chicken feet heading straight towards me as the food was passed around. Even though my stomach was churning, I politely accepted, and I watched myself chew as it turned to rubber inside my mouth.

1976-1986

I had been volunteering at a local neighbourhood centre. Just after Frazer turned two, I completed the Welfare course and began looking for a job. To manage my new life as a working mum, I prayed for part-time hours in the school term, a position close to home, and a Christian nanny. Not long after, I received a phone call offering me a part-time job as an assistant coordinator at the nearby neighbourhood centre. The family day-care centre gave me the contact details of a possible babysitter. During our meeting, I realised she had a son the same age as Frazer and, during the conversation, asked if she could take Frazer to church on occasions with her. I was overjoyed. Incredulously so thrilled that God cared about me so lovingly and had answered all of my prayers.

I worked for the Community Aid and Information Service. I felt it emerging within me as an innovator, forerunner, or however you might describe a pioneer. Each morning it would show up, ready to take on the world. I would unapologetically forge the way ahead and quickly tackle situations overlooked by others. Frail and the elderly didn't have anyone to do odd jobs for them, so I applied for funding so handymen could be employed to do minor maintenance. This eventually became a government initiative known as the Home Maintenance service. Then it was a matter of the elderly being isolated and could not get out into the community. After much prayer and endless discussions at a regional level, I felt inspired to draw up a list of those needing transport and another- a list of organisations that owned minibuses. My boss used this list to secure funding for further research, which eventually became the St George Community transport scheme. Many years later, it became one of the biggest in New South Wales. This was the beginning of my interest in transport and other local community needs. God was working, and I was flourishing. I decided that I did not have to be in full-time ministry to be serving God.

8

THE STORM

Two years later, I took up a new position as a Development Officer at the Canterbury Earlwood Caring Association. Earlwood had a high percentage of elderly residents and had been established as a soldier settlement after WWI. Over the next seven years, I enjoyed working in this caring community alongside my many volunteers. The more that worked closely with me, the better. In fact, I had one hundred volunteers working each six hours a week.

In late spring I and some others had founded an annual festival and we had a lot of fun coordinating it together. Over ten thousand local people attended and they enjoyed the many stalls and events. At this time of year, the weather can be sometimes unpredictable, so I prayed, and each year we had perfect blue skies. A Council Member told me he also planned their events at that time, because "the weather was so reliably excellent."

Together with a small group of volunteers the bi-monthly *Earlwood Community News* was published and delivered to just under ten thousand homes. We advertised our services in it and included many articles addressing local issues.

I was on the lookout for other community needs that required attention. Due to the elderly wandering off from our day-care centre and becoming lost, I helped set up the first centre for Alzheimer's clients in New South Wales. At that stage, Alzheimer's, a significant problem in ageing, was relatively an unknown condition.

We frequently made representations to the local Federal

Member regarding the needs there, and later, he introduced the Home and Community Care (Act) into parliament in 1985. Out of this legislation, many services such as the Home Maintenance Service and the Community Transport Service were established.

One day a local real estate agent came into my office and, discussed the elderly's inability to manage themselves while alone in their homes. He proposed a plan for a small retirement village. Later, he was instrumental in getting a government licence for a nursing home.

I could see up ahead the many possibilities for this community. One in particualr, was a need for young mothers to access, in print, all the communtity services available to them. So I prepared a booklet and called it *Children's Services*. My new neighbour, who had just moved into the area, told me just how helpful this was for her.

In 1984 I was awarded the Citizen of the Year for Earlwood. It was a surprise and during my speech I acknowleged the hard work of my faithful volunteers, for without them, especially Joy Golds, I could not have achieved all that I had. In the local paper's writeup about me, I read, *Earlwood is indeed fortunate in having such a dedicated woman as Marie who gives a deeper meaning to the word "Caring."*

In the interim, Doug and I planned to move to the Blue Mountains and build on the land we had purchased there. But after a change of mind, the land was sold, and the money was used to visit my family in England as my father had been very ill. Dad had his first heart attack at the age of fifty-four and was pronounced dead but resuscitated at the hospital. Every year after that, he had a major heart attack. After I received the baptism of the Holy Spirit, I wrote to him telling him that I believed God could heal him and that I would pray this would happen. After receiving that letter, he had another major heart attack and was hospitalized.

The cardiologist, wanting to do a bypass, told my father he

was not well enough. He was to go home, and if he had recovered sufficiently within three months, he could have the operation. The next day, he was lying in his hospital bed and felt something go right through his body. He assumed it was another heart attack of some sort.

My dad fobbed it off as unimportant. Three months later, he was back in hospital for the operation. When the cardiologist examined him, he said. "I don't know what has happened to you, but your heart has made a bypass all by itself." Miracles were a rare phenomenon for this doctor, and he was so shocked that he asked if he could allow his interns to meet my father. Of course, my father didn't tell them about the miracle, as he still had not put his faith in Jesus. For the next twenty-five years, he had no heart problems.

God was in the shadows drawing my family in on the other side of the world. This made their letters and phone calls all the more precious. Heather wrote telling me that she remembered me reading my bible and had bought one herself. She went to church on Christmas morning and a few weeks later when the vicar's wife visited her, she was converted. Some years later, when the vicar came to speak to her and her husband about the christening of their new baby, he also became a follower of Jesus.

Then my mother rang, "your sister Margot is dying before our very eyes, and we don't know what to do about it. Can you pray?" Margot had been diagnosed with liver tuberculosis, was only fifty kilograms. "Yes, of course, I'll pray," I promised Mam. The following week I went to a healing meeting at Bexley. "If anyone here has a sick relative and you would like us to pray for them, please come forward." So, I went forward for Margot and believed their prayers over me would bring healing into her body.

A short time afterward, her appointment with the specialist showed a normal liver. "Absolutely nothing wrong!" the doctor said. She had been miraculously healed. However,

Margot still could not believe that Jesus had died for her. So, I wrote a letter to the Pastor at the local Pentecostal church and asked him to visit Margot. "She'll become a Christian if you visit her," I told him. He led her to the Lord, and there was a dramatic change in her life. She eventually became a missionary in Romania.

After this, I took a job as a community transport co-ordinator. Under my management, the service was doing really well. I noticed the frail aged and people with disabilities were unable to get to their appointments. So I began piloting a scheme where they could be taken individually to their appointments. This became the first individual transport scheme in New South Wales. The Department of Transport was so impressed that interstate visitors were frequently brought in to view it.

I also developed an annual work plan and this was used as a model for all NSW community transport organisations. Our service was recognised as one of the most successful. Then, God took me through the most painful experience of my life. In the middle of this, I employed a driver. From the very start of the employment, the driver was out in the community spreading rumours about me. Even people who knew me very well started believing the stories - even though they were not true. In this sense trouble appeared out of nowhere.

So, while the services I was responsible for were thriving, the management committee could not see the driver was putting mud on my name. Much of the detail is not necessary to mention, but all to say, eventually I was brought before the Community Justice Centre. I was so sure I would receive justice there, but no, instead I was told, "It has been confirmed our opinion is correct and that you are the problem." During a time of prayer, I felt a cool breeze brushing across my barren heart. " Marie, I see great strength in you, much like a stalwart. You have what it takes to get through this. Stay loyal, work hard and be kind to those who are not supporting you. "

The Union was called and adamantly said the committee had no case at all against me. Even so, for the next three years, I was painfully harassed and experienced constant persecution. God told me that I was not to justify myself and not leave the job but stay there. I have never been through such a traumatic time. Even Christians were telling me that it must be my fault and I must be doing something wrong.

It is one thing to be unstoppable when everything is going fine; it's an altogether different story when obstacles are put in one's way.

But Douglas knew I wasn't the problem, and he continued to be a great support to me throughout the entire time. I would have found it very difficult to cope without him. I could feel my determination to get through this, yet my strength sometimes wavered. But strength is only ever tested on the weight given to carry. I learnt to accept the heaviness in my heart and persevered, and true to my stalwart nature, developed a greater capacity to be strong in trying situations. I held firm under incredible pressure. I would tell myself, *remember Marie, stay determined, and keep going. Even under tremendous pressure, you do not give up easily.*

I was determined to carry on unhindered by the chaotic trouble thundering around me. Every day, I got a grip on myself and refused to let this trial overcome me. I refused to let it affect the way I saw myself or the way I related to others. Instead, I went out of my way to show kindness when needed. And I, by my simple insistence, quietly endured and watched what God would do for me.

The endurance was arduous as it wasn't until three years later that God said, "You are free to move." Shortly afterward, the local council contacted me with some welcome news, "We have been watching all that has happened to you, and we know you are not the problem. We are offering you a temporary job to fill in for a worker going on three months long service leave." In that time, the worker retired and I was asked to apply for the job. My persistence under pressure was rewarded. I accepted the prestigious position and enjoyed a significant increase in salary. This showed me that God is no man's debtor!

A few months later, the woman who replaced me came to see me. "I am deeply ashamed of what we did to you," she said. "As soon as you left, it became immediately apparent that you were not the cause of the problem."

When I couldn't see what was going on, this trial taught me to trust God, and I did! I learned that He will never let us down in times of adversity and that if we leave the outcome in His hands, He will always vindicate us. Looking back, I felt my faith in God's goodness and His abilty to make things right for me, had become stronger during this difficult time.

During my years of suffering, Doug was going through his trials also. He had begun his Ph.D. and in the hecticness of life, had drifted significantly away from God. When Doug arrived in Australia, he found himself stuck in a religious system that had little to do with faith or a personal relationship with God. Instead of finding joy in Jesus, one had to find it in the world. Douglas was not a wishy-washy lukewarm person at all. He was either one hundred percent committed, which I remember only too well after his conversion, or completely uncommitted. In our early years of marriage, he was a powerful witness to me and others. Now, his eyes were firmly fixed on how other Christians were living their lives, and as a result, his faith was dwindling. He had hardened his heart and told me contemptuously, "Only people with half a brain believe what you believe."

His heartbeat grew louder

And I knew I must carefully follow the

master

The path started winding upwards

But it was still unclear

Exactly why God had

me here

1986-1996

9

HEAVEN TOUCHING EARTH

Ever since I was a little girl, I had this thing going on in me that if I wanted something, I was determined to get it. Typical of my stalwart nature, I would be willing to do whatever it took. I wanted to hear more from heaven and felt it would be life-changing. In the Old and New Testaments, people who wanted God's attention went without food. Some might call it a tantrum, but God calls it self-control. So, on Sunday mornings, I drove off to church without breakfast. Being caught up in the moment in worship helped me forget about all that was on my mind. So, I aimed at developing a heart of adoration when singing the songs.

As I listened to God, I heard messages that were intended for the congregation, and bravely I would give them. One Sunday, I felt God impress upon me a message about the potter and the clay. Pastor Steve, who was a prophet and a great encourager, confirmed that word to the church by saying that this subject had "exercised his heart much and that he planned to preach about it." Over the next four years, he taught on the prophetic and would validate everything God told me.

Then on another level, I was battling some of the childhood fears that still frightened me. I considered these fears "the left-over parts of me" that I refused to face. One day Doug came home with the idea of getting a cat. Nothing could I say would make him change his mind. "You'll just have to get over your silly fears," he said. It was the best thing he could have done for I had been conditioned to see cats as a threat, and I had no way of helping myself overcome this fear. In my Bible, "fear not" appears 365 times, one for every day of the year, so we never need to be afraid- even of the sort of fear we are conditioned to have. As I decreed these truths, my trust in God to protect me from illogical imaginings increased, and the fear dissolved.

Heaven visits earth

I was holidaying in Scotland with Margot when we heard of the news of a spiritual awakening in Sunderland twenty miles from her home. The pastor there had just arrived back from Canada and wanted to tell everyone about a new phenomenon occurring in Toronto. So, on the Saturday, we drove to the church to find a swarm of people outside a little hall. Inside there were no spare seats. People kept coming in droves.

When Ken got up to speak to the six hundred people sitting before him, there was such an expectancy in the air that you could hear a pin drop. It was literally like, *let all the earth be still before Him*. Ken made many attempts to speak but was so overwhelmed by God's Presence that he could not get any more than one or two words out. The entire room began filling with an unusual presence of peace, and with it came a sense of God's pleasure towards us. An inner joy started welling up, and some began laughing and couldn't stop. We later discovered that even those who were going through tough times felt refreshed. Indeed, this was hard to understand, but we knew heaven was touching our earth and God was in our midst.

The following week, back in Sydney at my church fellowship group, I told everyone what had happened in England. My life took a brighter focus towards everything when someone said, "If God can do it there, it can happen here." So, we all got in a circle and held hands and prayed, and two people instantly became full of the Holy Spirit. Within a month, Pastor Steve Penny took a group of people to Toronto, and everyone came back totally transformed.

My friends and I started attending the weekly 'catch the fire' meetings in an area an hour's drive from home where many people were physically healed and set free to worship Jesus more fully. We drove a round trip of 150km and often didn't get home until 1 am, but it was worth it as it felt like heaven had come into our worlds. Sometime later, pastor Steve moved to Queensland. I was devasted. It was at this time that God had impressed upon me to join the Mount Annan church.

When it was time to leave my spiritual home months later, Doug hit the roof. The Christian Growth Centre had been my life source for nearly twenty-two years. So, to discuss this matter with Doug was a big decision. "Don't be stupid," he said. "For twenty years, you pleaded with me to move to Sutherland so you could be near your church, and now only two years later, you are telling me that you want to go to a church on the other side of Sydney. You're not going, and that is final!"

What a dilemma! I was caught between obeying God and obeying Doug, and I knew both were the right thing to do. So, on a Sunday morning, I went to Doug and said, "if you don't want me to go to Mount Annan, I do know of a church locally." With this, Doug turned to me and very forcefully said, "Look, if God is telling you to go, then go to Mount Annan." Within minutes I raced out the door as I had an hour before the morning service began, and it was a fifty-minute drive. I felt God had wanted to see if I would adhere to Doug's wishes and as I had, Doug's heart was softened, and a source of great contention within the marriage was avoided. As it was, Doug never once complained at my travelling all those miles each week.

At a gentle prompting from God, I became friends with Sue Kennedy. Sue had recently joined our church; she was about my age and had also emigrated from England. We both shared a love for the disadvantaged, and in many ways, we were very much alike. We became very best of friends.

Marrickville Council

A pioneering spirit forges the way ahead when the path is unclear. It was easy to see where change is needed, but performing it at a high level of success involved going head-to-head at times. It wasn't without a battle.

My manager, directly over me, erected some very high roadblocks and often rejected my ideas outright. He made it hard for me to plan an initiative and to run with it. It didn't stop me though, as a teenager, mam appeared to be somewhat of a boss over me. It was her resistance during some of our most strenuous tug-a-wars that helped me the most. The more she pushed against me, the greater my determination to be stronger than her became. Back then, I took responsibility for what she downplayed, and right there, I had the map to follow in future years. If I was unstoppable then, I was more so now. So, I took responsibility for what I could see, which enabled many initiatives to be achieved. My performance reviews always showed I had all the insight needed to create change. The reviews pointed to a tremendous amount of work and some outstanding achievements in my final working years.

I had another boss, who from the sidelines thought I was a star player. He was there at every point, cheering me on. He nourished my visions and became overexcited at one of my biggest ideas - the implementation of accessible travel paths throughout Sydney for people with disabilities. It was a real game-changer, and he happily organised various meetings to implement this initiative. I worked very hard to achieve this and other ground-breaking dimensions within my various roles.

Among others, another hat I wore was a support role for the non-English speaking seniors. My colleague and I designed a gentle exercise class. It was the first of its kind, and after implementing it, we received a certificate of recognition from the Heart Foundation. To further support these wonderful elderly newcomers to Australia, I gained funding for their various programs. As a thank you, they invited me to their national celebration days. I treasured the variety of live music and delicious food at the Portuguese, Greek, Vietnamese, Yugoslavian, and Lebanese festivities. The Italian seniors - always seemed to be in a party mode and often extended their celebrations way beyond the festival days. It was such good fun.

Meanwhile, the accessible pathways plan was getting much attention, not only in my workplace but also from the inner west councils. Many other local committees in Sydney sought my consultation. Also, I worked with the Parks and Gardens in the local council and designed accessible play areas for children with disabilities and seating for the elderly. With this sort of success, I was asked to further research the idea of kerb ramps and easy access into public buildings.

Douglas could see there was little chance of my hectic pace slowing, so he thought a fortnight in the Bali highlands would rest my tired nerves. In the quiet oriental Ubud, we breathed in the tropical air and leisurely strolled through ancient rice paddies. The fascinating birdlife, ancient temples, restaurants, and oriental markets were every bit of what we hoped for and left a striking impression in our minds.

Then when I became interested in toilet designs for people with disabilities I was given the nickname "Toilet lady." While holidaying in France with Margot, I noticed an impressive design and scribbled down the particular model, make, and manufacturer. Then when back home, I contacted the company, and they happily sent me forty videos showcasing their product, and I then posted one to each local access committee. With God's guidance in it all, I saw the bigger picture of all of the possibilities to be attained.

I was happily devoted to my job and, over the years, gained a deep sense of joy at work. Yet, even so, I was becoming tired with the daily peak hour grind, as well as weekend trips to Mount Annan Church. Doug, who had retired four years earlier, wanted me to join him in his monthly meetings with the Australian Plant Society. But I found it difficult to add anything extra into my heavy schedule. It was all so exhausting. With a working life of forty years behind me, I began thinking about taking early retirement.

As the year drew to a close, I set about to finish off my various projects. Many were sad to see me retire, and there were lots of enjoyable farewell parties. On December 9, I went to my very last meeting at the Senior Safety Committee. During the afternoon tea, they were very complimentary. They said that Marrickville Council was way ahead of the other councils in collaborating and working with others. My main boss also made a speech in which he said, "Marie was indefatigable, she never missed an opportunity, and was a model worker." It was satisfying to know all of my hard work had been appreciated. More importantly, I had worked to the best of my ability as God's representative in that workplace.

Although I had relished my job, at fifty-eight years of age, I was ready for the next stage in my life and wondered what God might have in store for me.

But followed I did and listened I must

To follow the pathway, I would need much trust.

Work-life ended after forty years

The training continued in my later years.

1997

10

NEW DIRECTION

Change is something few of us are ready for or even like. But I was prepared to put my working years behind me and start a brand-new life. As I welcomed the New Year in, I sensed a new era stood before me.

Little though did I realise this new era would have me explore the world, its people and cultures. The taste of travel and my interest in helping people build better lives would merge into what today is now an international ministry.

In March, to celebrate my new freedom, Doug and I flew into Paris and set off southwards in our hired car. It had been many years since we had driven along the French countryside in springtime, and seeing the trees coming back to life after a hard-bitter cold winter was simply delightful. We revelled in the fresh, crisp air. The blossoming primrose, jonquils, daffodils and crocuses, and other springtime flowers were a sure promise that that summer was on its way.

We drove further south, all the while enjoying the sheer wonder of this beautiful place. Typically, Doug swung off main roads into quaint hamlets that hadn't changed in hundreds of years. In Arles, where Van Gogh lived, we spoke to the locals in our limited French and ate a magical dinner in the café depicted in the famous painting "Café by Night." Afterward, Doug followed an off-beaten track under a moonlit night to where we happened upon a daisy-strewn orchard, and there, we bunked down together. He always explored off beaten tracks and would have done so on his trip across the world to marry me.

Untouched by humans, the scent of beauty was everywhere. The following day we drove up a mountainous gravel road. So, upward we drove, and the higher we climbed, I sensed I would escalate from obscurity into a higher place of influence somewhere in the future.

We came upon a lake where the aquamarine sky rippled in the water and further up, the pretty primrose growing wildly on the side of the road seemed to be singing songs of happiness. Through onto a fabulous classic pink Rothschild villa, just one of the seventy-five luxury estates owned by one of the world's wealthiest families. Wealth and how it could be found in unlikely places intrigued me.

Then further on exploring Tuscany, where a lifelong dream to see the legend of the True Cross at Arezzo came true. Tickets were needed, and with the tour about to start, I raced back into town and returned in the nick of time. Climbing upon each rung of the ladder, I reached the heights of the roof and with my arm stretched out, touched the frescoes. It is the reaching up towards the heights in life, to the things that seem out of reach, that inspires my questing spirit.

After visiting the surrounding ancient Etruscan hilltop towns, as well as Florence's local fine arts culture, and Vatican City, we drove to the French Maritime Alps. Here Doug wanted to find a rare plant- saxifrage. Typical of Doug, for it, grows upon the highest point in rock clefts. We set out very early the following morning and drove up along the steep, crumbly narrow tracks. The gentle sun rays threw light on the sweet edelweiss and other exquisite flowers, but no saxifrage was seen. Right up there at a very high precarious spot, Doug said, "I'll do a three-point turn and go back a bit." As he did, eagles circled high above, and I watched on and prayed I wouldn't have to jump onto the bonnet to steady the car if the back wheels fell over the cliff.

We were up too high and the track too narrow to keep driving, so we parked and, on foot, came upon an enormous snowdrift. I was exhausted and, sitting on a rock, said, "I'll wait here for you." Two climbers stopped to have a chat. "Only hang-gliders come up here; what on earth are you doing? No one in their right mind comes up here." They looked at the bar of chocolate in my hand and my canvas-covered feet, "Especially wearing those sneakers. You must be crazy." Little did they know that up ahead, Doug was battling a snowdrift. Unable to go forward or backward, he thought he was going to die. But at dusk, my brave adventurer had gotten back to me at the rock.

A few days later, Doug left me at the local fete and set out again. He drove the car up as far as he could and climbed over a broken bridge. Up further, an avalanche had utterly buried the road in parts, and fir trees lay in tangled messes on the ice. But oh, the joy! He found the beautiful cerise plant, sitting completely unnoticed, blooming without an audience. He arrived back exhausted but happy.

Douglas's determination inspired me. If he could search so hard for a plant, I could also find the disadvantaged stuck between hard rocks. I had spent all my working life making situations better for some of the more vulnerable in our society. To help others find a better life was still burning, like a fire, in my soul. But I never imagined the people I would be helping would be speaking a foreign language in a faraway country.

Within an hour, we reached Annecy, a lovely alpine city with a river and canal passing through. It was there I felt to phone England. Margot anxiously answered. "Dad has only two days to live; come home right now." Feeling distressed by the news, Doug and I drove into Switzerland, where I boarded a plane. Douglas drove to England and met me there. Dad had all of his family around him and, being still alert, was thrilled to see me. We all reminisced about old times and were with him at 2 am when sadly, he peacefully passed into the arms of the Lord.

Mam was devastated. I stayed in England to support her through her grief while Doug returned to Australia. I had left home when I was eighteen and had only returned for short visits since. So, the time driving her into the countryside, exploring quaint villages, and having meals in beautiful old pubs was very precious and a wonderful bonding time for us both.

I arrived home to a disgruntled husband. Six weeks earlier, Doug had been enjoying a beautiful time in France with me. Now, he seemed to be going through a rough patch, and it didn't take me long to see that this was upsetting our marriage. On our trip at the rainforest, things got a little out of hand. Doug was having a horrid time being traumatized by leeches, and I was having difficulty with him. Our marriage was not going well.

Back behind doors, we were so mad at each other that we upsettingly discussed a divorce. He said, "I don't love you; I don't like you, and I don't want anything more to do with you." I turned to God, expecting Him to take my side in the matter. Instead, I was shocked when God said, "I want you to make Doug's life heaven on earth." To this, I thought, *I don't want to do this; it is too difficult*. However, my heart said yes, and I agreed. Although the path seemed impossibly hard at times, I stayed focused and found creative ways of giving him pleasure and making him happy.

Around this time, I was going through my own difficult stretch. This painful problem felt like a thorn piercing my heart. It began during the three months of isolation while in hospital recovering from scarlet fever. I tried making sense of why Mam didn't visit much. Feeling lonely and abandoned, I concluded she didn't love me, a heart-wrenching thought. Then God began shining His light into the long-hidden doubt I had about my mother's love for me; He gave me a picture of a garden and said, "*In that garden, the ground needs preparation before seeds are planted. If there are thorns or rocks or if the soil is hard, the seed will be vulnerable and cannot get the tender care and nurturing it needs. Your heart Marie, is like a beautiful garden and needs proper care, so the seed of patience, kindness, and gentleness and My love for you can grow deep within your soul."*

God gave me this picture to show the image of "unloved" was like a thorn, and a huge rock, preventing beautiful things from growing in my heart's garden. "It is not honouring to Me," He said.

So, Jesus taught me to replace those distressing thoughts with this healing image from Him, "You are my child, and I love you and cherish you, and I am with you always." In this way, I learned to overcome the loneliness I felt in that isolation room.

1998

Ardent Learner

Psalm 139 reminds us that God's thoughts about us are about as many as the grains of sand. Millions of them. If we are to experience the extent of these thoughts, we need to calm our minds and listen to His voice. I needed that calm for I had become very preoccupied with how in fact, God was going to use me. Surprisingly, right in the middle of bringing some calm into my heart at church one morning, the direction needed was given. It was as if God himself was speaking, "Indeed, I have a special plan for your life, and it will begin unfolding before your very eyes. You're in a time of training." So I promptly, at sixty years of age, signed up at Mount Annan Bible College. And this new direction culminated in my first year where surprisingly I became dux.

My desire to serve God had been influenced by missionary biographies. So I became interested when in my second year, the Bible College planned a mission trip to the Philippines. I prayed about joining them. Over a conversation with the principal, I decided to sign up. I started to get excited and wrote out my testimony. Yet, when I wrote the sermon out, I thought, *there is absolutely no way I will preach this. I'm happy to sit in the back row, out of the limelight, and pray.*

After all that travelling to get there, I felt sick and exhausted. It was a Sunday evening, and we were given two hours to unpack and settle in. Then we were sent out in twos, one to preach and the other to pray. Nonetheless, in a forced enthusiasm, I asked my friend Jenny who was going to preach. "Oh God will show us," she said loftily. *Ha, how super-spiritual,* I thought.

I had carefully folded the sermon and placed it in my bag. There was a big banner across the front of the church which said, "God always answers prayer." I was utterly stunned as it was exactly as I had titled my sermon. The impression that God directly leads is seared upon my heart. In fact, I began expecting God to show up in similar ways. During the trip, I learnt He would do this if I stayed very close to His heartbeat. I preached numerous times, and God was always there to give me the right words to speak prophetically or pray over people. I came home from this trip feeling completely confident that whatever the future held, I would be able to accomplish it with His help.

11

RETRACING STEPS

It is something of a habit I picked up many years ago when I had come out of a partying lifestyle. On the first day of every year, I'd spend on my knees, symbolically, and more so for listening than anything else. There were the usual standard instructions. God encouraged me to continue making Doug's life heaven on earth. He reminded me I was not to fill my life with soda pop but to put Him first in everything. He encouraged me to be loving and kind to everyone and bring my life to him each day, so He could prompt me in the direction He wanted for me. Then usually, there were some other interactions, and mostly I came away feeling uplifted and encouraged.

While I was busy studying at college, Doug was getting itchy feet and we began discussing his adventures in the Middle East. I had fallen in love with Doug's daring spirit, so it was exciting to take three months off and to be retracing those long ago steps. Of course, God had a sense of purpose in us backpacking around the Middle East. Unbeknown at the time, He was planning a life of high adventure in my later years, and travelling the world - meeting foreigners and involving ourselves in their lifestyle would put me in great stead for whatever lay ahead.

Turkey

The roaring touchdown into Istanbul shook us awake in time for the pink hues and beautiful early morning skies, a lovely reminder of our first sunrise together. Doug is a romantic, but he does not tolerate being taken for granted. He got himself into a heated argument with the manager at the hostel and was shockingly ordered out of there. The hotel next door had a magnificent rooftop terrace overlooking old Istanbul. It was everything we hoped for, and we spent most evenings relaxing over the exquisite views, happily reminiscing about each day with a drink in hand.

Of course, Turkey was a big part of Doug's overland trip many years previously. Now, he wanted me to be there with him as he recalled the colourful textures of this beautiful country. I had Turkish gozleme for the first time, and Douglas bought a banana at a stall. As we walked away, he looked at his change and said, "I've just been charged twenty dollars for this banana." By the concern on Doug's face, I could see he would not let this go.

Staring the stallholder down, Doug remonstrated, "I love your country, but you have cheated me!" But the man, reluctant to reimburse the money, argued back. Doug was adamant, and as they argued back and forth, a crowd gathered and began to chant, "Give him his money back! Give him his money back!" Very reluctantly, the correct change was given. To this, Doug straightened his shoulders and, in a very righteous manner said, "No, it's the principle of the thing," and walked off.

The next day at the spice markets, we enjoyed the vibrant colours and soaked in the aromas. We then later gazed upon the frescoes, stood in the tranquil atmosphere of the Hagia Sophia church, and explored other beautiful exotic landmarks. Then, to experience the authentic lifestyle, we travelled on efficient, reasonably cheap buses and began backpacking across the breadth of Turkey.

I had, for many years, known scholars had doubted the existence of the Hittites civilization. Yet this sort of antiquity has always fascinated me. So, to see an advertisement claiming their existence was more than I could hope for. Inside the ancient site, archaeological artifacts filled an entire village. It was as if I was walking into biblical times, Hittite language, enough to thrill my heart, was inscribed everywhere.

I was intrigued by the statue of a lion with the inscription "Aslan" at its base, as if discovering its origins from the C.S Lewis Narnia series.

I was quickly falling in love with the land that Douglas had tramped across to fetch me. After trekking overland, we caught a bus to a little town just short of the Iranian border. At Dogubayazit, we hired a taxi for a mere daily rate of $25 and explored the surrounding countryside. The area is full of wonders, a magical ruined castle and a vast meteorite crater were breathtaking. Then at Mount Ararat, I insisted on Doug taking numerous photos, for I needed proof at home that I had been at the site of Noah's Ark.

The taxi was speeding along towards another site when the driver noticed a group of his friends barbequing a goat. He pulled off to the side of the road. It's the sort of thing you do in the Middle East; stop and have a BBQ with your friends while showing foreigners around. Of course, we were invited, and to indicate friendliness and our open hearts, we used our relaxed postures and responsive smiles. Douglas with the men, and I with the women, we sat crossed-legged around the open fire. Mingling with the locals in this way, enjoying the mixtures of food, and hearing the various dialects, made it simply a fairy-tale day, and the memory of it still lingers on in my mind.

Of course, posh restaurants attract all sorts of people to their high-energy rooms. The ornate high ceilings and trimmings create the kind of beautiful ambiance seen in foreign films. The next night we were dining in such a restaurant. Across from our table were well-dressed ladies sitting with a very affluent-looking gentleman. Yet, the women kept disappearing and reappearing, and eventually, I realised that they were "ladies of the night." Douglas was sitting with his back to all of this and was unaware of what I could see. That man began his antics with me in a jolly mood, and I tried to ignore his glad eye. I just wanted to slide under the table. I couldn't ask Douglas to turn around and stare him down, so instead, I made an excuse to get us out of there, but our dessert hadn't arrived, so I was stuck. The man, who we discovered had a prominent position in the town, got up to leave, stopped by our table, and began speaking. Doug, totally unaware of my visions that I'd end up in the white slave trade, became more and more friendly with the guy. Eventually, I happily and hurriedly hustled Douglas out the door and back to the hotel. As if that wasn't enough, every evening army tanks patrolled outside our windows reminding us of how exciting it was to be in the Middle East.

It was almost midnight. Douglas and I had just gotten ourselves organised for the next day, when our door started shaking to a loud banging. We opened to find a frantic man speaking, "Be careful who you talk with; not everyone can be trusted with what you tell them." We had met him at the markets earlier, and he had come in the dead of night to tell us his story. As we sat over a cup of tea, we learned he was a retired school principal who had spent his summers in Turkey for the past three years building relationships with the Kurdish people. "After arriving, I would visit the poverty-stricken villages, and children would come tumbling out of their huts and take hold of my hands. Within a short time, the parents were also welcoming me," he said. "Did you ever become discrouraged?" I asked. "Oh yes, I was at the point of going home but I prayed and went outside and there in the heavens was a double rainbow. I felt that was God's seal of approval."

After an hour-long chat, he said his goodnights. We were inspired by his faith and in his stepping out and following God in this way.

12

THE CHASE

The Iranian border wasn't that far away from that hotel room, and I knew I would need a hijab. "There will be plenty of stalls selling clothes," Doug had told me in Australia. There was not a stall anywhere. So, standing in the queue, I began busily rummaging through my backpack. Muslim women standing nearby noticed my predicament, came over to me with the correct headgear and began to dress me with much laughter on both sides. Impressed at my hijab, the customs officer asked if we had any playing cards. We reluctantly watched him throw what we had onto the massive pile on the coffee table. Douglas and I never questioned the matter. Instead, our open posture meant that we would turn it into an adventure. Out of the blue, he said, "I'd like you both to come to my place and meet my family." Doug and I accepted the invite and, turning towards each other, winked. A perfect situation as we were keen to understand the Iranian culture.

The following day, the man's son arrived in a taxi to pick us up. On our way to his place, we could feel his unhappiness and discontent. By the time we arrived at his home, we had been told a lot about their lifestyle. As I walked towards the front door, I saw a silver dish further up in the garden and thought, *I wonder what that is,* and promptly walked inside. We enjoyed a lovely meal in their home and were surprised to find them western-like in their living. At the time of our visit, Australia had just lost against Iran in the World Cup Soccer finals, and wherever we went, they gloated, "we beat you; we beat you!" I was personally thankful for a country with so little joy, as this win brought the Iranians happiness.

The uniquely beautiful Middle East is very different from the West, and with few foreigners around, it's hard to remember another world exists beyond our holiday there. So, at Isfahan, a young American tourist was boarding the plane also. Having met her previously, she was easy to spot in the crowd. After touch down, she said, "Come to my hotel and enjoy the facilities, and let's spend some time together." We had booked into a grotty backpacker's hostel, so yes, of course.

After unloading our gear, we stood outside the Abbasi Hotel gazing upon its glorious grandeur. The steamy hot water splashing our dry skin in the ornate bathroom was delightful. We sat in the luxurious hotel room eating exotic fruit and then, later on, swam in the Hollywood-type crystal blue waters pool, all of which felt quite decadent to us.

Being from the north of England, tea drinking is part of our culture. But it was under the tall arched bridges in Isfahan that we had a completely different experience. In the famous Tea Houses built into the arches, it was exciting to walk along the vibrant Persian carpet into a darkened, evocative room. Eastern music filled the air, and brass ornaments lavished sideboards. Elderly cross-legged men were sitting on cushions smoking hookahs while we soaked up the moment, sipping Iranian tea - a moment we would treasure for years to come.

Then, we experienced further glory relating to strangers at the ancient mud-brick city of Bam, where we met a mystic Sufi dressed in a long flowing white robe. During our conversation, I noticed his rings glistening against the striking spectacular pink sunset - it was enough to entice us to stay and talk long into the evening. But reluctantly, as the sun faded behind the horizon and disappeared into a misty grey evening, we said our goodbyes.

Doug and I loved getting out of our comfort zones. Trekking and roughing it was our idea of fun. The one downside to this was the lack of laundry, and as a result, I washed our clothes in bathroom sinks. My imagination went wild when

I discovered a sign "washing facilities available." But that excitement was short-lived as the "facilities" were nothing but a mere plastic basin perched on a cement block in a public courtyard. That night, I sat with the moon high in the sky, plunging my hands in the cold water, tears coursing down my cheeks, washing our clothes, and longing for some home comforts.

We had been to Tehran and Shiraz and had walked around the ruins at the Persepolis - where a magnificent palace had been built over 2,500 years ago by Darius the Great in 551BC and burnt to the ground by Alexander the Great 331BC. We were now on our way to an Iron Age site. As we sped along a dusty road in the northwest of Iran near the Iraqi border in a shared taxi, we listened to three Iranians speaking amongst themselves in Farsi. Then at our destination, Doug apologetically squirmed past a passenger who responded in perfect English, "Be very careful. Not everyone understands." Oblivious to its meaning, I stepped out into the blazing sun, straightened my blouse, and turned towards the relics.

I could hear Doug breathing in the stifling air, and more so, his boots crunching into the dust. After casting our eye over the ruins for quite a while, we began to leave. Out of nowhere, we heard the sound of a jeep coming up over the hill, speeding towards us. Our hearts sank as we watched four huge black-bearded men alight and, with folded arms, stood staring us down. With the nearest village five kilometres away and no way of rapidly leaving, we tried diffusing the situation by waving and calling out "As-salaam Alaikum." Our Arabic *"peace to you"* didn't work. Doug, thinking this might accelerate badly, said, "Let's get down the hill as quick as we can."

We glanced over our shoulder to see the jeep speeding away and two of the men following us. So, we quickened our pace; they seemed to be gaining ground. *I'm in God's hands;* I reminded myself. I caught my breath as we neared the main road; the men were close behind. Doug was edgy, and mercifully, out of nowhere, a little old egg van came chugging around the corner. We jumped out in front of it and asked for a lift. "Hop in," he said. Doug, quickly, with his dusty boots on the front seat, leaped over into the back. *"How rude!"* I thought.

As our driver accelerated away, the jeep sped from around the corner. The four pairs of eyes followed us onto the very edge of the town when they, thankfully, gave up the chase. We both settled upon the idea of being more astute and aware of our surroundings. More significantly, we were only to take ourselves into situations where transport was available.

Even so, we loved backpacking and connecting with these amazing people in their magical world. We then travelled by bus out of Iran towards the Turkish coastline and stopped at Goreme in the scorching heat of Cappadocia. This area is significant to christian history, but notably, there was little christian activity at the time of our visit. Nonetheless, this area is fascinating, full of geological formations of tufa stone known as fairy chimneys. Many of these natural rock formations had been made into tiny chapels and were adorned with beautiful frescoes.

The heat was near suffocating, so thankfully we found a hotel built into a cave. I loved the idea of staying in a cave and immersed myself in its cool, relaxed ambiance. The proprietor offers to do our laundry in his washing machine. I was ecstatic and gave him every scrap of clothing that I could lay my hands on. Hours later, he came back with a bedraggled bundle of wet clothing and a very soggy passport that had been left in my jacket pocket.

It was the interactions we had with the locals that made our trip ever so memorable. After our washing machine drama, we met a friendly man selling beautiful Persian carpets, and after some happy discussions, he invited us to his home.

Commonly, after a meal, we all sit around for a chat. The old father, in typical Middle Eastern fashion, asked Douglas about his manhood. "How many wives do you have?" The answer was obvious. "Just one wife," Douglas said. "I have four wives," he boasted.

The man didn't know that Douglas was much more of a man than most. He had walked across the breadth of Turkey, faced growling wolves, extreme temperatures, and overcame many lonely hours walking towards his bride and a bride, mind you, who was sending him letters outlining her doubts about marriage.

He is my hero, and far be it that he needs four wives to prove his manhood. He is my braveheart and I am delighted to have him as my own- always by my side.

At Ephesus, we stayed near what would become a world heritage site in 2021 - the magnificent ruins. As our feet strolled along the dusty red earth, we passed the lady with wings - the goddess of victory and other archaeological ruins dating to 4000BC. It took more than five hours to view the Odeon theatre, and the extensive remains of the streets and temples and the sheer size of the ancient library were impressively overwhelming.

A stone relic pulpit took my fancy, and I conjured up an image of me preaching high on the little plinth. I spoke about my hope to help the needy one day, which, little did I realise, would mean traveling to a foreign country.

The early church in Ephesus was passionate and diligent to walk in righteousness, and sometimes this meant exposing evil - typically a christian thing to do. But their hearts were so busy serving God they had shelved a closeness with Him. Jesus had been their first love, but now, no longer. While John, the beloved disciple was exiled at Patmos, he heard Jesus' thunderous voice. There in that tiny cave, he was given messages to send out to the various local churches.

Jesus spoke to the church in Ephesus first.

"These things says He who holds the seven stars in His right hand, who walks in the midst of the seven golden lampstands. I know your works, your labor, your patience and that your cannot bear those who are evil. Any you have tested those who say they are apostles and are not, and have found them liars; and you have perservered and have patience and have labored for My name's sake and have not become weary. Nevertheless I have *this* against you, that you have left your first love.

Remember therefore from where you have fallen; repent and do the first works, or else I will come to you quickly and remove your lampstand from its place - unless you repent." Revelations 2:1-6 NKJ.

Jesus wants a close relationship - not distant devotion. It was a constant challenge to me - to put Him first in my life.

13

REPAIRED RIFT

Whatever the situation Doug and I are facing, we have this unspoken trust in each other that we have what it takes for it to turn out alright. So, bring on the challenges, we'd say.

I came across a bookshop and discovered a surprise. Inside were Christian books. Upon seeing my interest in them, the storekeeper declared her faith and invited me to attend a meeting in the bookshop that evening. At dusk, leaving Doug in his comfort zone, I stepped into a surprising twist where I found the bookshop all locked up and to be in total darkness. Thinking I must have mistaken the time, I bravely waited in the dampening night air. An hour had passed, and I noticed, in the distance, a couple standing under a street light.

They eventually approached and asked me if I was waiting for the meeting. Feeling relieved, I said, "Yes, I am." They then told me that the storekeeper had suspiciously thought I was a foreign spy and cancelled the meeting. The couple disclosed to me the fear in which the Turkish Christians live. Even though Christianity is allowable in Turkey, in practice, it is another story. As we spoke, I heard of the flourishing life they had given up in the north of England to teach English and support the struggling church in Turkey. I felt challenged by their tangible passion and admired their surrendered unselfish commitment to follow the Lord in this way. It's hard to imagine living in that sort of realm.

When in a shared taxi on our way to the airport, I was sitting next to a hostage negotiator, which prompted our experience in Iran. Seizing my moment, he told me they would have been looking at "taking you hostage in the hope of easy money." In a miraculous split second, we had escaped that fate. Other situations could have been dangerous, but God's guidance and protection during those unexpected twists showed His promise to be trustworthy and reliable. The truth that lo, I am with always had been my anchor of hope on this trip.

With reluctant hearts, we sadly said goodbye to these beautiful people and their country and boarded a hydrofoil to Rhodes.

Greek Islands

We stepped onto the wharf at this ancient crusader city, and after unpacking in our hotel, and eating lunch, we strolled along the streets cladded with old medieval buildings. Rhodes had not changed one bit and for three beautiful days, we were swept back in time—a most cherished feeling of ours.

From Rhodes, we island-hopped to Crete. In its capital Iraklion, our accommodation was far from salubrious. All night long, the ancient lift creaked up and down. We discovered to our chagrin that we were staying in a bordello, so we quickly moved out the next day.

Doug had worked in Crete, and even though it was many years ago, he was keen to visit the seaside village where he had been stationed. It was a gorgeous experience, leisurely soaking up the ambiance and dining in beautiful idyllic seaside restaurants.

In the middle of our boat trip over to Santorini, the winds began whipping up into a raging storm. During the entire six hours, Doug was inside, happily buried in a book while I was outside tossed about in the pelting rain, violently seasick.

At Santorini, we stayed in a Bed and Breakfast owned by a Greek family, and happily they invited us to their little boy's christening. After the service in the tiny church we met all their family and friends during an exuberant celebration of loud music, dancing and singing - a wonderful hallmark of Mediterranean culture. Often we in the West think quiet music is more holy. Ramping up the emotions or quietening them in the kind of music we listen to, both have a place when celebrating.

Getting out of Santorini was impossible but it barely mattered being stranded there for the next six days. Santorini is the island of my dreams. Little beach restaurants served us taramasalata caviar dip, one of my favourite foods, and strolling amongst the whitewashed cottages with blue-roofed churches was a holiday to remember. Looking out upon the azure seas and the spectacular caldera was just breathtaking.

On the Sunday, I attended a Greek Orthodox Church. As I listened to the liturgy and watched the priests in their robes swinging incense holders, I began inwardly criticising the prolific icons and incense. My thoughts were interrupted with the Holy Spirit's stern rebuke, "Don't you dare criticise My people. You can only see on the outside, I with My piercing eyes, can see the heart, and there are many who love me here," He said. It was an excellent lesson for me, as a critical spirit is something I have had to contend with and allow God to deal with in my life.

Greece

With my Australian passport still drying out and thoroughly unusable, I was grateful to have my UK passport with me. Itwas late at night when eventually we flew into Athens. Doug described the tiny hotel room as "a coffin swarming with mosquitoes." We had hardly slept fighting off those voracious vampires, so we rebooked. The new accommodation had fantastic views overlooking the Acropolis. I had learned about this famous historic site years ago in school, and on our way to exploring it, we passed by a tiny Cycladic village with whitewashed cottages and blue roofs. The Parthenon was breathtaking.

On the Sunday, I worshipped in a Presbyterian church and witnessed three Iranian men being baptised. It was so exciting to see what God was doing, especially since I had first-hand experience in Iran and had seen how persecuted the Christians were there. My heart sang with joy throughout my time in Greece.

Egypt

Cairo was a late-night touchdown. All the guide books indicated caution about touts. We caught a bus into the centre of town. Being on our guard and feeling very smug with our heightened sense of awareness, we got talking to a "very nice man," who, a school teacher, wished to improve his English. He said to us, "Of course, I know exactly where your hostel is, and I can show you how to get there." So, Douglas and I got off the bus in the pitch black of night and followed him through some of the backstreets. Looking puzzled, he said, "Oh, I know of a better place, and a taxi would be quicker."

In the back of the taxi, we were both feeling entirely shattered by hunger ad a very long day. Suddenly, we became startled to hear cars and motorbikes roaring and coming at us in all directions. Convinced we were in a riot, we felt unnerved by it all and quite frightened. Later we found it to be nothing more than a friendly spat between two rival soccer teams that had been playing a grudge match and were celebrating. After all of that drama, "our friend" took us to a hotel that cost five times what we usually pay and demanded money for his services!

What a night! It was 2 am when finally we fell into bed. But even at that very late hour, both extremely tired and very hungry, I produced a book, "Far from the Madding Crowd." Although exhausted, Doug too, was interested in this book.

"That's mine," he said, "and I want to read it." "No way," I said, "this is my book." A blazing argument ensured. This was finally resolved by Doug tearing the book in half and giving me the front bit. For two days, we toured Egypt in silence. Indeed, not a good Christian witness on my part.

We had booked into a very run-down hostel, and we were the only occupants on the fourth floor. The following morning, I felt it safe to go to the bathroom in my nightie. On coming out, I froze mid-step for there, like wild mushrooms springing up after a downpour, a group of men on their knees praying had sprung up in front of me. I was mortified and dashed as fast as I could to the safety of the bedroom.

Overt worship is a big part of daily life in the middle east. In my heart, I am overawed by the wonder of creation. I adore the God of heaven and earth, the One who made everything including the sweltering days in Egypt and the icy cold in nights there. But we never got used to the sudden change of temperature at night. Having left our warm clothes at the hostel that morning, we froze through the *Sound and Light* show that evening as the sphinx told its story—a small price to pay for such enduring memories.

On Sunday, I set out on foot to find a place of worship, and after walking for hours, stumbled across a French convent. They were delighted to allow me to worship in their chapel, and I spent a happy hour alone with God.

Doug and I eventually repaired the rift and found peace with each other. To celebrate, we booked a two-day trip down the Nile on a luxurious boat called "The Glory." We stopped at fascinating Egyptian temples and had afternoon tea at Old Cataract Hotel where Agatha Christie wrote "Death on the Nile." Such luxuries were a blessed relief from the two months of roughing it, and we soaked up every minute of its glory.

14

THE FLUTE

Unstoppable people know it is either adventure or safety, one or the other, rarely both. I chose adventure and expected safety to follow. It was the thrill of the situation and never knowing how it would turn out that gave me the greatest joy in life. I learned this as a child. Danger and trouble were adventurous games to me.

In distant Iraq, the sound of war was rumbling. Next from Egypt, we were travelling an eleven hour bus journey into Israel through the Sinai desert. Being aware of the situation was hair-raising, but more so exhilerating - for gun-toting guards would be escorting us in their jeeps.

From its inception, Jerusalem has been the centre of much political and religious animosity. A few days after arriving, we were strolling through the old city when suddenly confonted with some shocking news that all British citizens were to evacuate immediately due to an impending war.

Amid the noisy tumoil on those normally quiet narrow streets, we hurried back to our rooms and there, sipped on our hot tea. Sipping hot, freshly made tea is what I had seen done during a crisis while growing up, and chatting about options was another. After our discussions, we thought it best to leave; our family would be worried after all. Yes, much better we catch a flight out.

Moments later, as I typically do in a crisis, I laid my hands on my Bible and prayed. *"Lord, you brought us here; what do you want me to do?"* I opened its pages and turned to my reading for that day. "Stay in the city," I read—a direct instruction. Out in the streets, residents, and only them, lined up for gas masks.

Foreigners were not given masks. It's not the sort of thing Doug and I carried with us either, but I did own a mask once. A long time ago. Without a mask, it was not safe to stay. We tried calling the Australian embassy, but it was the weekend, and we got a very laconic message virtually saying, "She'll be right mate, ring on Monday." So, after some deliberation, we stayed for even though we didn't have a mask to save our lives from toxic gases, we did have a word from the Lord.

Within three days, the emergency had blown over. In this dangerous situation, we felt God's presence to be very present, for that is what He promises in troubling times.

In the beautiful streets of magnificent Jerusalem, my heart was moved so many times, in fact, everywhere I turned. It was an exceptional experience to visit Mount of Olives and the Garden of Gethsemane, the site of Jesus's betrayal. As we walked along the Dolorosa, the same cobblestoned path Jesus had trodden towards his crucifixion, everything was more than I ever imagined it to be. Those unforgettable emotions still linger to this day.

On our final Sunday, at the "King of Kings" Pentecostal service, I sang my heart out in the sheer joy of being in Jerusalem. Sharing worship with God's people was a fitting climax to my stay.

Jordan

It was hard to say goodbye to our little bit of heaven. On our way to Petra, we drove through the Negev Desert. As the scorching sun seared the bus windows, I looked out towards the campsites sprawling with Bedouin goatskin tents. We heard water was a scarcity, yet the Bedouins had settled there for centuries. On personal reflection, our flourishing years can dry up even for the best of us and our lives can feel like a hot scathing desert. I thought back to those who had given up on their walk with God and who had settled for places of lack. Yet, like the Bedouins, how easy it was to stop and set up camp without the faith to press on towards more extraordinary things.

Then on through the freezing night, reaching Petra just in time for the pink hues to gladden the eastern skies. Near the famous Treasury building, the exquisit colour rugged donkeys and camels were waiting to carry tourist through the narrow sandstone gorges. Doug and I climbed up on a nearby hill and stood, beholding the distant caves cradling us. Back on the ground, I surreptitiously joined myself on a guided tour, and there, happily ran into some friends from Australia.

At dusk, Doug and I walked to the end of the valley and climbed a pinnacle overlooking misty blue mountains in the distance. There, to the sound of a lonely shepherd playing his flute we sat drinking sweet, smoky Bedouin tea. That night sleeping out on the rooftop, we woke to see the sky lit up and laying there were engrossed by the beauty of a stunning meteorite shower. Then, when all was quiet, those mellowing flute notes came wafting across my mind, and I wanted to stay in that moment forever.

The glorious red earthed Petra was our last stopover in the Middle East and, as such, sadly meant the end of our four-month holiday. Back at Aquaba on the hostel's roof, we stretched out on mattresses and set our gaze upon the glistening stars, too mesmerized to sleep. Back at Cairo airport, with our memories full of treasured high adventures, close calls, and many God-given appointments, we regrettably climbed aboard an Australian- bound plane.

15

THE TEST

While putting the last of our dinner plates away one balmy evening, Margot called and said, "Mam is in hospital. She has pneumonia." I rang the hospital, and the nurse put me through, but mam was too confused to speak. So I spoke to the nurse again, only to find she had suffered a stroke. Immediately, feeling overwhelmed with stress, I packed my bags and prayed mam would be okay. The following day, I was on the first flight out of Sydney. After a very long flight, I arrived into a blizzard and the devastating news I had not reached her in time.

In the middle of my sadness, the magical snow laden streets and colourful celebrations turned my thoughts back towards home with Doug and the boys celebrating the presents under the tree without me. Mam's funeral was held on Christmas Eve in a beautifully scented church. Every pew was packed to the brim with people who dearly loved her happy personality and zest for living. She was not only loved by her family but also by many of her friends and acquaintances. Being a Christian, we knew that she had gone to be with the Lord and reunite with Dad in heaven.

**

It was good to be back in the classroom after the Christmas break. My future ministry was something close to my heart, and often I questioned God about it. Usually, when we pray these sorts of prayers, we think about doing something tangible, the kind of notable thing others can see. But often, I had been shown the most extraordinary thing I could do for God was to make my heart ready for Him to use.

As one of my final assignments at Bible College, I was to

lead a praise and worship session. The worship leader led each morning students in a time of adoration before God. Then it was my turn to lead. I did aspire to lead an amazing session, but only God knew that. I was bitterly disappointed because there was no sense of God's presence, and we just sang a lot of songs. Later, when alone with God, He said, "You have a competitive spirit, and I will not move so that you can be better than someone else." It was a firm rebuke.

Motives run very deep and for God to touch them is painful. It wasn't that I wanted to win; it was just that I wanted to be better than everyone else. That there is no room for competition in the kingdom was a lesson that I needed to learn.

Around this time, I began feeling a prompting to follow a unique path specifically designed for me. This would include a hill for me to climb. From this moment onwards, I felt God say I was now on the upward path. The Bible has a lot to say about the kind of paths we walk on. Some paths can take us off track, and others can help us reach places we never imagined. The path that God had me on was a path that would lead me toward an end goal, a satisfying outcome. He could see where He was taking me, and He alone knew the best way for me to reach the goal. There were specific tests along the way that I would have to excel in or at least pass, and I knew His voice would travel with me. This made it both easier and other times harder- for the lover of my soul did not let me get away with much.

As the end of my third year at Bible College drew to a close, I began praying that God would show me the next step. In another assignment, I researched the needs of the area. This led me towards focusing on Mount Annan Church Community Services (MACCS). At the time, it was barely functioning. Happily, my very good friend Sue was also being led in the same direction as me. Sue and I decided to walk around Mount Annan's area to pray and seek God on the path we should be taking. We both felt the prompting to set up a budget counselling program. Neither Sue nor I had any experience with this, so I approached Saint Vincent de Paul Society, seeking permission to sit on in their classes. They were most responsive. For the next two months, I quietly sat in a corner observing the budget counsellors at work. Not long after that, we modelled and set up something similar.

We then prayed for volunteers to help us and clients to receive from us. Within days needy people were on our doorstep. Shortly afterward, we applied for financial assistance to help with the client's electricity, gas, and water bills. Many who came for counselling did not know God as their father, and we took the opportunity to share that He cares about them and knows about every area of their lives. We could see God's hand upon those outside the four walls of the church, and as we prayed, many were moved to tears.

Meanwhile, Sue set up a program ministering to ladies in need, and I became involved in a food share program where quality bulk food was distributed in $20 bags and sent out to various areas. To facilitate these programs, the church gave us a small room on the church property. A large refrigerator (to be stored in the room) had been donated for the frozen food. Sue didn't like the space it took up, and we clashed over the ownership of the room. I was adamant that the area had been given for MACCS and that the food share program had been part of this. Two very strong-willed women going head-to-head was not a pretty sight. Each of us wanted to do God's work, so we learned to settle the matter God's way, and our friendship blossomed.

Airds was one of the two high areas that we hoped to help. It was a local government housing area full of low employment and other high-end needs. We began sensing that God wanted us to set up our programs there. We contacted the Department of Housing, which was impressed with our upcoming trajectory and offered a building for our offices.

For an annual fee of $1, we now had a home to set up our rooms for budget counselling and other such programs. After much success, we began branching into Claymore, the other high-risk, high-needs low-income area. Claymore meant sword and had a prophetic destiny. If they only knew they were destined to use God's word as a sword to fight off the problems that so quickly arose in that place.

At the end of 2001, during Christmas lunch Graham's friend called with news that the road to Bundeena was about to close due to a raging, out-of-control fire in the area. The Christmas pudding had just been served, and without taking another bite, Graham's entire family raced out the door and sped off. With only part of the road closed the next day, Graham decided to stay and guard the house. Meanwhile, his wife Wendy, Hannah, our two-year old granddaughter, and Wendy's parents, Tove and Gunnar, returned to stay with Doug and me until the fire abated.

16

A CALL TO FAITH

It was New Year's Day, and as usual, I sought the Lord. I felt Him tell me to continue making Doug's life heaven on earth. I was also to continue praying for the family and seek His face for prophetic insight. He reminded me not to fill my life with 'soda pop' but to put Him first in my life. He encouraged me to be kind and loving to everyone and that despite being sixty years old, He was preparing to take me to a new level of faith. God is always telling me, "Marie, you are in a season of training and preparation." While settling, these words also created sheer suspense, and I was excited and often wondered about His plans for me. I knew whatever I did; it would be out of my love for Jesus and not out of trying to win His.

Doug came to me not long after I had this conversation with God and said, "I am more in love with you now than I have ever been." I smiled back at him and thought of the times I stuck to my goals, and now, God had turned my marriage right around.

Doug and I still wanted to travel to India. Our trip previously had been cancelled due to the 9/11 terrorist attack, but even now, all our planning had fallen apart. I eventually realised that God was stopping this trip. So, being the flexible sort of people we are, we invited Margot to visit us. Her work in Romania was constant, and she needed a break. I discovered that Qantas had an excellent offer with frequent flyer points; you could fly around Australia with five stopovers.

What a great opportunity. So, I booked Margot and myself a trip around Australia. We flew to Tasmania and met with my cousin's wife for the first time. From there we flew to

Melbourne where we enjoyed some time with my son Mark. Onwards to Perth, a little south at Bunbury, we swam with the dolphins and enjoyed a fantastic whale cruise; they were diving under the boat and swimming alongside us. The native flowers in Western Australia are world-famous, and we spent many happy hours perusing them. At Uluru, we enjoyed the "Sounds of Silence" dinner in the desert and ate under a brilliant canopy of stars hanging so low that we could almost reach up and touch them.

Finally, crystal clear beaches, toad races at the local pub, and fantastic markets at Port Douglas - a perfect final stopover. The church, a tiny white clapboard building with incredible sea views, was one of the prettiest I have ever worshipped in. God has certainly created a beautiful world for us to enjoy.

We finished our holiday with a day of prayer and meditation. God spoke to me about using my faith when needing finances to support my church's ventures. I didn't realise this at the time, but God saw within me a great faith...I only saw it as a wavering faith. He would often remind me, "Do not look to people or expect them to meet your need. I wasn't to be overcome by fear. I want you to look to Me alone and not to the circumstances surrounding you. In this way, you will be building up your faith muscles. God finished by saying, "Is anything too hard for me?"

He warned me about looking to second causes, and He wanted me to use my faith to look to him alone. "Prayer big or small prayer. Nothing happens by accident." Jesus said. I began pondering upon in fact, how nothing happens by accident and that everything is all part of His plan.

He told me that I was not to look to man for wisdom, as man, without His help, can never understand His truths. Instead of expecting man to help me find answers to my problems, He told me that He is always in control, and I was to look only to Him for spiritual enlightenment. He said, "I will never ask you to do anything I cannot do; I will always give you the power,"

Further to this, He would tell me. "I want you to have a servant's heart and serve people, touching lives with My love."

God has piercing Eyes, and with them can see deep into our souls. He knows us more than we know ourselves, and He cares about our souls even more than we do. But He is very gentle. When handling the innermost being, He knows the delicacy in which he made the heart and soul. His skilled words can bring significant change.

He went deeper into my soul and told me that in the hidden recesses in my heart are dusty cupboards. He asked permission to clean them out, and I knew He was referring to my angry thoughts and wrong motives. He asked me to examine my thoughts and sort through them, sifting out the good from the not-so-good. "Impure thoughts require rigorous examinations," He said. He wanted nothing in me that would disturb my spirit. He went on to say that I needed openness to what He was telling me so I could allow Him to challenge my thinking. He was teaching me to trust Him in challenging situations. Little did I know that God was preparing me to face a situation bigger than the greatest of all tests.

***

The year had flown by quickly; Douglas with his projects on flower identifications and I had been busy volunteering at church. By the end of the year, Doug, who had always been a very fit man, began to complain about feeling constantly tired. He also had pain in his back. At first, we thought he had strained his back lifting a heavy log, but he decided to go to the doctors when it persisted.

Our family doctor, who knew us very well, ran some tests and said there was an anomaly. He referred Doug to a specialist, who identified a low blood count and an enlarged spleen. A week later, Doug's count had dropped a further 5%. We were beginning to be concerned. On December 21, he went to see a haematologist, who prescribed Prednisone, saying sixty percent of cases would recover with this treatment and another forty percent would indicate the presence of leukemia. What a dreaded word. Another appointment was made for January 7. We decided to put everything aside and enjoy our Christmas with the family, little knowing that this would be his last Christmas with us.

2003 was my 'annus horribillis.' In February, Doug was finally diagnosed with leukemia. This was a tremendous shock for us. It was not only so heartbreaking that Doug was given this diagnosis, but almost simultaneously, Mark was diagnosed with a severe allergy, and the doctor told him he could do nothing about it except put him on powerful antihistamine tablets. He was placed on a stringent diet and was not allowed any colouring at all. He was eventually given prednisone, but the allergy reappeared every time he tried to come off it.

In May, when my niece and her husband came for a short holiday, we did not let them know Doug was sick, in fact, we tried to make life look as normal as possible. It is the sort of thing Doug and I do when facing challenges, the other during such times, is to make things exra special. It was Jan's birthday, and to celebrate, we took them sightseeing and ended up at the beautiful seaside suburb of Watsons Bay, where Jan and Matthew dined in for lunch at the famous Doyle's restaurant.

Doug and I played with their kids on the beach and ate fish and chips. Jan and Matthew had a lovely time alone and came back raving about the meal, saying it was one of the best since their honeymoon. That night Matthew took Jan to the Opera House while we babysat two very excited little boys who barely wanted to sleep. "Let's play," they'd say.

So guided by the street lights, I took the boys to the swing park. They came home exhausted.

Around this time, Frazer had decided to resign and travel to Central America. So, in August, he cashed in his Yahoo shares and set off. Mexico was his first touchdown, and he stayed with a family there, intending to learn Spanish. Somehow, he lost all of his credit cards, and the bank took ages to sort this out. The following month, he fell down a deep ten-foot hole in the dark and cracked a vertebra. A rickety old kombi van cum ambulance transported him to the hospital. It sounded awful, and we began to make plans to travel to Guatemala to bring him home. We prayed much for him, and within a couple of weeks, he was discharged from the hospital completely recovered. Thank you, Lord.

17

MEMORIES

At the beginning of November, Doug noticed a rash, and his toes became discoloured. At that point, the doctors gave us the devastating news that his condition had progressed dangerously. He went to see a leukemia specialist.

"This is a very nasty disease, and there is no cure," he sadly said.

So, our only hope was in God healing him. Mark and Graham came to us and offered to give bone marrow to their dad, but the doctors said he was too old for it to work.

I had started to plan for Christmas, Doug brought home the fresh pine tree from the local scouts, and we decorated it. That same week, we also went to the Royal National Park, where he took photos of the flowers for the interactive CD. But by this time, he was not strong enough to carry his camera equipment, and I had to help him. He recently admired a painting at a local art show that I bought as a surprise Christmas present.

At the end of November, he was admitted into the hospital for chemotherapy and was told this would extend his life by at least twelve months and at Christmas would discharge him. Over the past three years, Doug had been working on an interactive CD of plants on the Coast Walk, ably helped by a group of very knowledgeable ladies who assisted him in identifying the plants. While in hospital, he worked on his computer, processing the slides and showing the nursing staff the photos he had recently taken in the Royal National Park.

Early into December, we were told that he would be very

vulnerable the coming weekend because his white cell count would be very low. He had one nightmare of a day when he was in great pain. The nurses would not give him any analgesics inferring that he was making a fuss about nothing. Finally, after much pleading, they gave him two Panadol.

Frazer rang to see how his dad was and offered to come home. "I'm okay, just continue with your holiday," Doug replied. Based on this, Frazer went off to a small island where he was uncontactable.

Doug's veins had collapsed shortly afterward, and the weekend staff didn't have the confidence to cannulate him. So, the medication wasn't given. I was distraught that Saturday evening and insisted that someone give him the much-needed medication. But it was too late. On Sunday, I spoke to the nurse about how upset I was with the treatment, and she suggested I make a formal complaint.

I was with Doug the next day when they began moving him out of his ward into the Intensive Care Unit (ICU) as he had pneumonia. He looked towards me with his beautiful, gentle eyes, blew me a kiss, and winked. Then he disappeared down the corridor as they wheeled him away.

In ICU, Doug was put on a respirator, and the doctor said that only ten percent of people survive. At this stage, he also said it was important that the immediate family be informed.

Mark and Kate had just gone to Brisbane on holiday and had only been there one day when I had to phone and inform them of the seriousness of the situation. Immediately, they caught a plane back to Sydney, and Graham came up from Bundeena.

Doug was in a coma, but the nurse told me that he would be aware of us and that he could hear our voices. I held his hand and kissed him many times. I told him that I loved him and that God loved him. I also told him of the story of the thief on the Cross and how Jesus said, 'this day you will be with me in paradise.' I told him that God wanted to do the same for him.

At 3 am the following day, we got the dreaded phone call to come to the hospital immediately. We all spent those next few hours by his side. Just after sunrise, his favourite time of day, at 6.20 am, Douglas peacefully passed away. God had promised me many years ago that He would restore the years the cankerworm had eaten. I clung to that promise trusting God that in those last days and hours, he had indeed re-surrendered his life back into Jesus' care.

Doug and I had collected many beautiful moments together, and in countless ways, these memories held much comfort. They reminded me of of all our happy times together and of all the exciting things we did. In another way, it made my loss even greater.

So, during these difficult days and for most of 2004, it was hard to control my sadness. Frazer, who could see my struggle, decided to stay at home and support me for a few months, for which I was eternally grateful. As we took down the Christmas tree early in January, I thought back to when I hoped for a few more good years, but now he was gone. I felt utterly unprepared for a life without my darling by my side.

Graham's friend Nick worked as a journalist. In an obituary for Doug in the Sydney Morning Herald, he wrote to emphasize Doug's love of plants and his involvement with the Australian Plant Society. It gave me great comfort to see him acknowledged like this.

To keep Doug's memory alive, we asked one of Australia's foremost artists in Bundeena, Jai Wei Shen, to paint us a portrait. Jai Wei used a photograph we had of Douglas setting out on his overland journey to Australia.

We also had our names inscribed on the Welcome Wall for migrants at Darling Harbour. And more specifically, we left a message in the remembrance book at the cemetery.

"He lived a life of adventure, love, laughter, and friendship in the pursuit of excellence." It was a comfort to me to keep Doug's memory alive in this way.

The days were hard. I felt I had lost my right arm, we did so much together, and he did a great deal for me. To everything around the house that needed doing, he would say, " Leave that, I'll do it."

Overwhelmed with sadness, it was hard to move forward. It was only last year, Doug was still playing Rummiking with me, and how I loved playing this with him. So, in January, I tried socialising with our regular group of friends. There were eight of us playing Rummiking in two separate groups. I asked to play with the ladies because playing with men without Douglas was just too much. After everyone went home, I realised that it was still way too early for me to be getting back into life.

With the sudden death of Doug and now, Kate's mother extremely unwell, Mark and Kate hastily decided to be married. It was a small wedding with only some of Kate's family in attendance.

Then I had some recent photographs developed, and as I glanced through them, I saw a beautiful photo of Doug at our youngest granddaughter's Name Day party in October. It was the very last one of him. Memory after memory came flooding back.

It was easier to be in places without a constant reminder of Douglas, such as the Church's Food Share Program and the Budget Counselling. I could concentrate.

In February, I began to feel vulnerable after a bout of painful tendonitis in my right foot and then shingles. I realised it would be only a matter of time before Frazer left and how defenceless I would be on my own.

Our three-storey house needed a lot of maintenance, and it was a fair distance from Mount Annan. I discussed moving closer, and the boys agreed that it was the best option. I began investigating and found a beautiful three-bedroom villa under construction near my church.

18

EDELWEISS

Over the years, Doug and I have taken many photos, and many of them are tucked away in a big box. But it is the photos stored in my heart that I have enjoyed rummaging through the most. Today was one of those times, for it was our wedding anniversary, and I was alone in the empty house and desperately missing the love of my life.

As I looked through my favourite memories, I thought back to the first day we said our vows. That day's happiness was palatable, yet there were no phone calls from the boys, and I felt they had forgotten this special day. However, Graham surprisingly arrived the following morning with a massive bunch of the prettiest flowers. This was yet another beautiful thing done for me to be stored forever, never to be forgotten, safe in my treasure chest of memories.

Shortly afterward, Mark and Kate came up from Melbourne to join us for a trip to the coastal walk which Doug was so fond of. Along the coast walk, we stopped at a sparkling pool and scatted some of Doug's ashes, and each one shared some of the most precious times they had with him.

I placed the house on the market with a Christian real estate agent, and it sold within the first week. As the villa was unfinished, I put my furniture in storage for the next three months and booked a flight to England. Then, taking all my happy memories with me, I sadly farewelled our lovely home in Gray's Point.

In August, I took Doug's remaining ashes to where we had our very first kiss. As sad as that was at Charlie's Garden, being with my family in England was just what I needed. My sister Margot was lovingly supportive. She had organised for us to do lots of lovely things together, including a visit to

Buckingham Palace and a night at the famous Globe Theatre watching Shakespeare's play "Much Ado About Nothing."

After arriving home, I relocated to Narellan and moved into my brand-new villa in the Angus Bristow Retirement village. Doug's portrait came to me a little while later, and I promptly hung it in the dining room. It was such an incredible comfort. Throughout the day and frequently during some lonely nights, it was a beautiful reminder of him - one that brought many smiles and much solace to my heart.

Throughout the years, it was a grand family affair celebrating Doug's birthdays. And now, to be blowing the candles out without him was so painful. Amid the heartache, my family and I had lunch at the Botanic Garden's Restaurant. We all ate and remembered Doug's constant search for hidden treasures in the outdoors. Doug had kept the family's spirit of adventure alive and was the love and heartbeat of my life. I desperately missed him.

Then the hardest of all to remember was the week of his death. On that terrible day, December 16, and the week following his funeral, I spent in a flood of tears.

With fresh sadness at my loss, it was time to put up the Christmas tree. So many memories came flooding back. Doug's tradition was to buy a fresh tree cut from the forest, and I wanted to do the same. Getting it home from the shop was a big problem for me, but I managed. I set it up as I had seen Doug do so many times. Some friends came around and helped decorate it. I then stabilised it by attaching the top of the tree with string to the nearby curtain rail. Then we left for church. On my return, the string had snapped. To my horror, the tree had fallen over and left a substantial brown stain of muddy water on the cream carpet. Later that night, in a panic, I rang the carpet cleaner.

"I will be around early tomorrow morning," he said.

After seeing the stain, he sighed. "Oh, I don't know if I can get that muddy mark out." My heart sank.

He did his best. In fact, it came out perfectly, and I was so pleased. But that was the last year that I had a freshly cut Christmas tree.

***

After the Christmas tree drama, I faced each new day, courageously wondering if anything else would come up that I couldn't handle. As I bravely met each day in the new year, they were becoming manageable, and the boys were busily getting back into their routines with work and family. It had been hectic too at church, which helped me adjust somewhat in a better fashion. I began facing each day more confidently.

In June, it had been twelve months since Douglas and I were at Doyle's celebrating our 39th anniversary. As we finished the last of the dessert that night, I had no way of knowing the family and I would be meeting here by ourselves a year later. Even though it was a bitter-sweet time, I tried to fill my 40th anniversary with memories of our joy and happiness throughout our married years.

Robertson was one of Doug's favourite getaway spots. To celebrate his zest for life, I met with some of his favourite friends from the Plant Society. The memories came flooding back as I walked on the creaky floorboards into rooms where I almost could see him standing by the quaint windows as he often did. And us both gazing upon the high ceilings from our oversized bed. I remember how, on cold nights, we'd sit together by the log fire and snuggle up and how we'd go for long walks during the wintery days, enjoying spectacular views and being enchanted by the birdlife. It was a bitter-sweet week and was yet again reminded that life is full of both rain and sunshine.

It was now November, and I was surprised at the pace at which the year had passed me by. Graham and Frazer took me out to a favourite restaurant for Doug's birthday. Their support certainly helped me get through a difficult day. Then on the second anniversary of Doug's death, Graham, Wendy, and the girls came with me to the cemetery. I laid a single red rose on the memorial book with the message, "My one true love. I will love you forever."

Doug's four-wheel drive was too big for me to handle, so we had given it to one of our friends from the plant society. Graham and I wanted to visit a favourite camping spot of Doug's near Bathurst, and we needed Doug's old car, so we borrowed it back from her. That day, as we drove out from the city up into the clean mountain air, I thought of the man who walked his way across the world to marry me —so many memories. We stopped for an apple strudel at Schwarz's Bakery Wentworth Falls, Doug's usual. Over coffee, we lingered and reminisced about happy times.

We then drove out through Bathurst onto a narrow crumbly road known as the Bridle track. The native plants and smell of dust brought back a flood of memories. Suddenly, my eyes became aware of a huge four-wheel drive heading straight for us. With a quick swerve, Graham barely missed the edge of a deep precipice. A heart-stopping moment! But typical to our Irving style, we both laughed and said, "How exhilarating was that!"

I thought back to the many of those "roller-coaster near misses" Douglas and I shared. We had come on this trip to find the exact spot on the Macquarie River where, thirty years previously, I had gone down the rapids backward. The kayak spun sideways and became trapped between two rocks while it filled with water. I was petrified and screamed until Doug came to rescue me. The sheer excitement of life on the edge with him brought joy to my heart. That, for a moment, was pleasurable, and Graham and I finished that day feeling it was all so much fun.

But the pain of my loss felt eternally persistent. God saw the grief in my heart, and He knew how to soften its rawness with little treats along the way. One such pleasure was a visit in March from my old school friend Mary. She and her husband Colin had been in New Zealand and were now with me for a short holiday.

To celebrate old times, we had an unforgettable degustation lunch at Tetsuya's Restaurant. Rated fourth in the world, these world-class fourteen courses were a once-in-a-lifetime experience. As I sat tasting the delicacies, I was reminded of the little flower edelweiss, a sweet little bloom usually found in the Swiss Alps on barren mountain heights. Its charming beauty is a pleasant surprise to the toiling climber. I thought of my own toil during times of loss and sadness. This little flower represents a wish of elegant times that bring renewal and a fresh start. To me, the degustation was, in fact, a touch of hope amid my painful experience. When going through tough times, such experiences are there for all of us if we only notice the delights that come our way and gather as we go along.

PART TWO

19

INSPIRATIONS

In 2006 my *dark cloud of* grief was hanging low over my life. To lift it, I thought of all the happy times Doug and I had while overseas together. It was now my decision to travel, and my fascination with the work Isabel Kuhn did with the Lisu people helped me decide. There was an advertisement in the local paper for a trip to the Burmese border in southwest China. *Oh, that's interesting,* I thought. I decided it was time to fulfill this lifelong dream and visit the Yunnan Province. So, at 68, I set off by myself, joining a tour group.

The trip started with drummers and ethnic dancers at a Chinese wedding in Kunming. The trumpeters handed out sweets and cigarettes as the bride in white arrived in a stretch limo – a typical combination of traditional and modern customs. Then, the bargaining over mountains of bean curd, animal heads, and many other exotic such things at the markets the following day wasn't a pretty sight. My big test, though, was a three-day trek to the Tiger Leaping Gorge. It was a challenge, as I, the oldest member of the group, found walking hard and I became exhausted to the point of nausea, almost vomiting. Some of the younger ones were happy to help me up to the top to see the magnificent view, and I was so thankful.

All the while, my mind was on getting to a church on the weekend. So, I told the Chinese guide, but he poured scorn on the entire idea.

"There are no churches in China," he said.

"Oh yes, there are," I replied.

After some discussion, he finally agreed that I could go off on my own to find one. After hours of searching, I was on my way back to the hotel; very dispirited, I whispered a prayer.

"Lord, if you want me to go to church, you are going to have to show me."

I was out walking again, when, as if God did in fact show me, I looked up, and right there in front of me was a sign "Merry Christmas." So, I strode through the front door with a dictionary in hand and was told of the following day's service venue and time.

The surprisingly quaint church was quickly filling up when I arrived, and the singing began. The entire service was in Mandarin, and being familiar with some of the tunes, I sang along in my heavenly prayer language. At the end of the service, the sound of English wafted past me, and I could see some young ones speaking fluently. So, I asked them.

"Is there anyone from the Lisu? "

"Oh yes," they answered. "That young man over there is our worship leader. His grandfather helped the first missionary J.O Fraser translate the Bible into Lisu." I was introduced to this young man, and after speaking with him, joined him and others over lunch. I was surprised, moreso dumbfounded but, even so, thoroughly delighted that I would be speaking with a close connection to J. O Fraser, one of my favourite missionaries whose stories gave me some of my greatest inspirations. Afterwards, two young people from the Lisu tribe prayed with me. A double blessing and a highlight of the entire trip. God exceeded my expectations.

We finally reached Beijing, and I said a fond farewell to the travel group and started on a thirty-four-hour train trip on my own to help out in a children's home. At the end of one of the train's rattly corridors was a self serve area - hot water dispensers, plastic bowls, a packet of noodles, and to make everything perfect, sleeping carriages for the overnight trip. I shared the sleeping quarters with five Chinese nationals, all speaking Mandarin, except one who became my interpreter. I took out my travel Rummiking, and soon we all joined in laughing together. The Chinese love games and they are very good at them. They were all new to this game, yet, I was somewhat mortified when they all thrashed me.

It was a surprising first few days, for although the children were all well cared for, it was apparent they lacked nurturing. You can imagine my distress seeing the children, most of whom had disabilities, were all eligible for adoption; only two out of ten were in the process of being adopted.

Before boarding the flight to Beijing, I had given away the last of my Chinese money, expecting to catch a meal on that flight, but no food was served. My connecting flight to Sydney was delayed, and I was famished, having not eaten all day. Sitting next to me at the airport was a young Chinese girl, and I struck up a conversation in my broken Mandarin.

"Oh, I can speak English; I am from Australia," she said. As we continued chatting, I learned she was a Christian and had just come from the very same bible school I had been to in Dali. She had been brought up in a Christian home but now was in a crisis of faith. She needed to know for herself what it meant to be born again and commit her life to Jesus. I shared my journey of faith, and this proved to be a divine appointment. When we had finished talking, she reached into her backpack and pulled out some food.

"I don't suppose you are hungry?" she asked.

God is a God who sees and, being such a Person, saw my dilemma and provided the right solution to solve my problem. I thanked my friend and boarded the Sydney-bound plane.

ON MY OWN

I had travelled to China with an organised group, so I thought I would try venturing further out by myself. The following year, just as winter was setting in, I closed my front door behind me, and I was on my way to Zurich. Due to fog at Sydney airport, the plane was delayed by three hours, which meant I would miss all my connections. So, I spoke to the booking clerk.

"There is a connection I have to catch in London." I gasped.

He responded, "Our partner British Airways, is leaving shortly; I'll book you a flight with them and inform Bangkok airport of the change."

However, in Bangkok, they wouldn't let me back on board.

"The flight is fully booked," they said. I argued with them and landed in the manager's office.

'So, what's going on?' he asked.

"I will miss my connection to Zurich," I frantically answered.

"How would it be if I gave you a direct flight there?" I thanked him profusely.

The direct flight gave me extra time to visit Zwingli's Church - an early reformer and then I joined a boat tour where I met a local resident. We instantly became friends and I was shown the local tourist spots. That day's sightseeing and her kindness were a rainbow and showed me that some flurrying storms have more than one sign of God's goodness.

The following day, I took the most breathtaking train ride

to Milan. In a compartment with a charming Swiss family with three teenagers, I spent a couple of fun-filled hours laughing over a game of Rummiking. We tried spotting the sparkling cobalt blue lakes, snow-capped mountains, and flower-filled meadows in between our turns. Then, after we were all giggled out, quietening myself, I sat close to the window and swayed along with the train winding its way around the Mediterranean coast, passing ancient villages. And in that quiet moment, I began dreaming of all that could be ahead of me.

Finally, we arrived at the tiny village of Bonassola, and I booked into my hotel and later met up with a walking group. On foot, we strode along a track that took us past five villages nestled in cliffs overlooking the azure Mediterranean Sea. As we paced ourselves through the Cinque Terra, I felt like I was in seventh heaven. It was astonishing to follow the Via Dell Amore (lover's path), past brightly coloured cottages, gazing down at the colourful boats bobbing about in the tiny harbour way below us, and frequently stopping at quaint cafes for lemon sorbets.

Back at the hotel, I was handed a postcard. It read,

Marie, the Australian with a walking group in Bonassola, and a tile from my Rummiking set stuck to it. I was most surprised, for how it reached me, I will never know.

I was in my element, having the time of my life. In Rome, walking through the catacombs where the early martyrs were buried, I contemplated their horrific deaths and their willingness to be eaten alive by ferocious lions rather than disown their King. At the Colosseum, I felt emotionally challenged by these brave souls.

I followed other ancient monuments, most of them almost two thousand years old, and then came upon the Trevi Fountain. I stood watching as many hopefuls threw coins in, hoping they'd meet their true love.

I had been warned of the dangers of being an older woman travelling alone in foreign countries. "It isn't safe," they'd tell me. Of course, they didn't know my zest for adventure and my trust that everything would turn out alright, so they had no option but to look on with concern.

From Rome, I travelled by train to the beautiful Amalfi coast. I arrived at Sorrento late at night only to find my private room at the hostel had been let out. To my horror, I was placed in a mixed dormitory, and was led to a bunk bed. "There is no way I can climb up that broken ladder," I said. The manager took all the belongings from the bunk below, stashed them on top, and said, "okay, you can sleep there."

The following day the receptionist gave me the key to my original private room. I was just about to unlock the door when, inside the room, I could hear a man's voice. I fronted the receptionist and said, "I don't mind sleeping in a room with three men, but one man on his own! No way."

'Sorry, I've given you the wrong key,' she said.

But it was too late; I'd had enough. I walked up the street and booked into a hotel. At the beautifully breathtaking Isle of Capri, I walked out of the crowded town and very soon was on my own, revelling in the beauty.

After this Italian idyll, I was on my way to England to visit my cousin Margaret who had been converted a few years previously. It was not uncommon to be in a church and never hear that Jesus died for your sins, and my cousin Margaret was one such person. But at a Billy Graham crusade, she heard that Jesus died as if she was the only person on earth and she was given the gift of faith.

After her conversion, we enjoyed each other's company all the more. We both enjoyed walking, so one day, we took her neighbours' dog for a walk. The river was flooded and to our fright, the dog jumped into the raging torrent. We cried out to God and grabbed a big stick and managed to get him to bite into it, and we pulled him back onto the bank. In all of this excitement, the precious camera Doug had given me before he died went missing. Retracing our steps, I was devastated the camera was nowhere to be seen. I reported it missing to the police and thought it would never be found. Then out of the blue, I received a phone call reporting my camera been discovered by a lady out walking. Overjoyed at the person's honesty, I couldn't wipe the smile off my face. "Lord, I should have trusted You more."

Then at Margot's, the two of us spent my final day hoping to hear personally from God. Already...like many times before, God had spoken to us both much about our impatience and sharp tongues, two sins of which we were both guilty. But it wasn't all bad. We were encouraged to be shown our hearts are dedicated to Him. Margot had a picture of me as a sunflower reaching up to God, always looking into His face. A great way to end a fantastic holiday. I knew that God was calling me up to another level of faith, where I would be financially supporting a feeding program for children. I was being called to follow him one step at a time.

Meanwhile, back home at Mount Annan, I always offered to pray for those seeking help in the budget counselling. It was a special touch for them, a surprising one too. For many had no idea just how much God felt about them. As tears trickled down their faces, it was as if God Himself was speaking from heaven directly into their hearts. Afterwards, I could see their postures had relaxed as if they had just been touched by tangible peace and profound love. It was a holy moment and very heartwarming to see many being cared for in this way, especially those suffering addictive lifestyles and unemployment.

21

THE MAP

A short time later, I was given this word.

"A new level of responsibility is yours if you speak about God's wonders." I was unaware that teaching His truths would eventually become my life's work.

In Hudson Taylor's Journals, I found the roadmap for those with a pioneering spirit. It was all laid out and I desired to take the same direction and live the same lifestyle - a life lived for others. As such, I decided to dedicate a trip overseas each year to serving God in any country of His choosing. A group from our church were travelling to a children's home and visiting a prison in Mozambique and I decided to join them.

Though aware of a pioneering spirit within me, I am also aware of my ability to ask for God's help when needed. Such was a time when I was about to visit a prison. I got before the Lord and told Him that I had no idea how to relate to a prisoner, and he reminded me of Paul. "Tell them about my right-hand man who had been a murderer. Tell them that there is nothing they had done worse than that, and as I forgave Paul, I would also forgive them."

The following day, I spoke with a man at the prison and told him about Paul and the message of the hope God wanted him to receive.

Then, at the children's home, I had another lovely surprise. Joy is something we felt the moment we walked into the room, but surprisingly, it was so infectious, we joyfully joined in with the children dancing and praising the Lord. Later that week, a friend and I went to work in the babies' ward. On our arrival, an Israeli cameraman from the famous

700 club was filming a documentary on the effects of short-term mission trips on young people. When he saw us in our sixties, he decided to broaden the documentary to include the impact on young and old. This eventually was screened worldwide some months later. In many ways, I sensed that my trip was a training for the days ahead. I stepped out in faith and loved all the many new things I was learning.

***

God warned me about Sue's failing health, so I took the information to Pastor Rohan. He approached Sue and felt it right to tell her that I had been given a word that she was putting herself in a dangerous place. She listened and recommenced her medication.

A couple of years later, a very punctual Sue was very late for work, and I was asked to check on her. As I drove up and saw her car in the garage, my heart sank. I unsuccessfully tried to push open the locked door and called Pastor Rohan. The fire brigade came, and it seemed Sue had had a massive stroke. I was devastated. It was hard to accept she was gone as we had worked together for many years. She was my very best friend, the one I turned to if ever I had a problem.

As the weeks disappeared into months, I missed Sue all the more. Especially on Monday mornings, she would come around to my place at 11 am, and we would pray together. Then after a quick lunch, we would go for a walk beside the river. This had been our pattern for some years. It was a special touch to a busy week, and now I didn't know how I would survive without her.

I knew Sue was in a better place now and that we would have a great reunion one day. But through reading the scriptures, I felt the promise of His Presence with me during my time of distress.

After receiving Immanuel's comfort, it became apparent that every time I read a Christian book or listened to worship music, I invited Jesus into my world. God was trying to teach me to rest in His Presence, a place of surrender and a place of letting go. It would be there He could come and pour His love into my stilled heart before Him. But while I liked that idea, I did have other plans.

God told me that if I wanted to hear His plans and the specific way He would lead me to achieve them, then I would have to spend time in His presence and walk in a posture of dependence on Him. Prayer was becoming a gentle tug-a war between me and God. For He also knew I wasn't interested. He knew up ahead He would prise my hands off the steering wheel, but for now, He watched on at my fierce grip on the plenty of plans I had for myself. He knew all about the time I spent focusing on them, and He knew all about the other prolific strategising going on in my head. Every time I closed my eyes to pray, my mind began filling with new ways of improving this or ideas about changing that. Like Martha, Jesus would often say to me, *Marie, Marie, you are troubled and worried about many things.*

***

Many of my friends dropped by the Saturday before my seventieth birthday and celebrated over cake and tea with me. It was a happy time of relaxing together, and I was especially encouraged to be given a prophetic word that *my next decade would be the most fruitful of all.*

Frazer had flown in from England, and on my special day, Mark and his family came from Melbourne. After lunch, my three lovely boys and their families and I dressed up for an afternoon tea at the Intercontinental Hotel. Some occasions are great; this one was exceptional.

Then, on a perfect summer's day later that week, my boys and their families and I travelled to Green Patch on the south coast. It was a gorgeous quiet beach with a campsite close by, and it was lovely watching the grandkids play so well together. We snorkelled, kayaked, and boogie boarded. At night, while the kangaroos freely hopped about, we sat around the campfire, eating toasted marshmallows, and amidst much laughter, I watched as the boys played a hilarious game of cards.

It was such a memorable way to finish off the celebrations. Having all my family around me was such a comfort and very important, for they are a source of great joy.

2009

I had been praying with the clients after their budget counselling interviews at Claymore. However, the new coordinator of the community centre was not happy and threatened to make an issue of it. I stood firm, saying that I was a volunteer and the clients were always happy to receive prayer after seeing how much we cared for them and certainly after receiving financial assistance. I stood firm and didn't buckle under this pressure to abandon my esteemed values. It is something we all need the courage to do, for in a day when standing out by standing up for what we believe isn't something we cherish doing. Most like to disappear into the crowds where they do not have to own their beliefs. Even so, I spent most of the year seeing lives changed through our many programs at Claymore.

At our church's annual Easter Conference, the keynote speaker spoke on God's glory and linked it to God's character and presence. This ministered to me, as I felt God wanted His character to be seen more in my life. I knew this was essential for me to seek his presence and power in an added deliberate way through a deeper relationship with the Holy Spirit. How persistent God was at bringing me into this beautiful dimension of faith.

***

In September, I was in England and feeling thoroughly spoilt. As a National Trust member, I enjoyed visiting historic houses and magnificent landscaped gardens. Oh, the sheer elegance of Wimpole House - a beautiful Georgian manor near Cambridge, owned by the daughter of Rudyard Kipling, the author of Jungle Book.

Frazer was living in London, and together we decided to go to a Berber camp in Morocco. I have always wanted to ride a camel in the desert, and I felt pretty snug in between the humps. That was until my head nearly hit the sand as the camel got to its feet.

The young twenty-year-old girl, who was in charge of the camp, seemed drawn to me.

She said, "I am a very spiritual girl; that's why I come into the desert to meditate."

"Well, I am a very spiritual woman," I countered, "and I have found the way and the truth and the path leading to life. Jesus said, if you are looking for these things, He is each of these." Her interest was tangible. Again and again, she sought me out to know more.

In my travel book, I had read that the stars could be seen so much brighter just a short distance from the camp in Morocco. So, I asked Frazer to come with me on my first night in the desert, but he said he was tired and wanted to go to bed. I did want to see those stars, so I decided to go by myself. As I walked out of the camp, our guide saw me and asked where I was going. He said, 'wait, I'll come with you.' I was glad of his company, for I imagined he'd know a lot about the night sky. Up on the top of the dune, I began to think it wasn't the night sky he was interested in after all. He produced a blanket.

"Let's just lie down here, and we will see them much better."

Some adventures have invisible obstacles and to overcome mine, it was on for young and old. "I am just a poor camel boy who had no prospects of being anything else," he said. I began to realise that he thought I was one of those silly old western women who thought she'd have a fling with a young cameleer. I jumped up, saying that my son would be very worried about me and that we must get back. We started down the hill, and once again, he produced the blanket and said, "Let's just stay here for the night."

Oh heavens, I thought. *How am I going to get out of this predicament?* I looked up and sighed a prayer, "Oh Lord, I have been so naive; I am sorry."

Again, I stressed how worried my son would be if I did not arrive back at the camp soon, so reluctantly, he folded his blanket, and we were on our way. When I got back to our tent, Frazer was fast asleep. "Weren't you concerned about your mam?" I asked him at breakfast. To which he replied, "Oh no, mam, you can look after yourself!"

"Yes I can, of course! But you should have come! You'll never believe what happened last night," I said.

2010

Back in Australia, my long-time friend Robyn and I were concerned that our church lacked a discipleship training program. It came up over a meal while holidaying together, and we decided to pray about it. That is when I heard God say to me, "Well, you do it then." God and I discussed my getting involved, and typically, He won as heaven had just voted that I would run the program. Then to settle the matter further, Robyn broke the silence and said, " God just told me I have to do it."

In my early days as a Christian, I was impressed that the Antioch group had helped me manage my fiery trials and overcome my fears. They taught me that God's word is powerful at disarming things from the past that frightened me. Each week I learned a verse and recorded it in my little book and met up with my mentor. I was also expected to attend a home fellowship and a Sunday service.

This training gave me a rock-solid foundation to withstand the trials of life. It would be now about forty years since I had seen that book on the other side of the world. So, I prayed God would help me find it. I felt a prompting to look in the old brown suitcase in the garage, for that is where I felt God say it was. I opened the case, and lo and behold, there it was, sitting on top of a pile of books.

Robyn and I used this verse book as a foundational basis of the discipleship course. After completing the draft, we took it for the pastor's approval.

"Most certainly, that looks to be a solid rendition of the way forward," he said.

The transferring of the soul into the kingdom of love requires work, it involves deliberate action. I always knew that. It requires a change in the way we think and an adjustment in the way we feel about God and the world and the relationships we find ourselves in. It requires a nurturing of the soul, an embracing of the new covenant and living a life steeped in abundance.

The program was successful, and many new Christians joined our group. Over the first several years of the course, we saw many of them go on to be firm believers. It was such a privilege to be involved.

Still upward the path led me to a land far away

To a group of people

who begged me to stay.

22

THE INVITATION

Not long after this, news came in from Margot that we both had been invited to Kenya to visit her previous pastor. God knows my ardent interest in missionaries, but I thought it strange as he and his wife barely knew me.

Happily, I arranged to meet Margot in Dubai. From there, we travelled to Kenya for a brief two-week visit. The bustling traffic and colourful clothes, and dusty streets in Nairobi all gave a mixed message. But take an eight-hour drive into the country, and the message is very clear. The locals were not doing so well.

We told them of our desire to help over the following weeks. "OK, let's go for a drive to a nearby village, and the local school might need some help," Pastor Harold said.

At Rafiki village, concerned, we listened to the principal, "Hunger is a special problem. Many children come to school hungry, unable to concentrate. Often, they faint, and many risk starvation and die before they reach five years. Other children are unable to attend school for they are out searching for food with their families."

By the devastated looks on our faces, the principal could tell Margot and I were distressed and perhaps might want to help. Striking the iron while hot, he quickly asked, "Can you ladies start a food program for the children?"

"Of course," we happily replied. "We can provide the finances if the school gets the food and employs a cook," we said. So, it was agreed upon. The one hundred and twenty children from the kindergarten class would daily be given a mug of maize porridge known as Uji.

The night before we were due to begin the program, Pastor Harold received a threatening phone call from a man who said, "We know you are devil worshippers because the children are fainting at school because of you. If you go to the school tomorrow, we will firebomb your car and the church." He wasn't fazed, and told the man he would not give in to his threats. We went to the school the next day, and the feeding program began.

He then also organised a visit to four of their local schools and two Sunday schools. I have never seen so much dirt on a classroom floor nor a room so bare. The children looked up from their exuberant faces- obviously excited to listen to our Bible stories and colour in a picture – many of them had never even held a pencil.

Over lunch, Pastor Harold casually mentioned that he wanted to develop a module for improving the livelihood of the locals. He couldn't wipe the smile off his face when I mentioned my previous work as a community development worker. He later phoned Bishop Martin and said, "I think we have found the person to develop the training module."

I loved my time in Kenya, and I was very reluctant to be saying goodbye so soon. Margot and I flew out to Dubai, and then I caught a plane to Amman in Jordon and then a bus to Jerusalem. Robyn, who had flown over from Australia, was waiting for me there. We happily stayed close to the Jaffa Gate in the old city at the New Imperial Hotel, a charming old hotel overflowing with Palestinian artifacts.

The following day, we met some American students from a Lutheran bible school who stayed in a separate section at the hotel. They were on a world tour, visiting seven countries and learning four languages. Over the next few days, we spent a lot of time over meals getting to know them. Robyn and I shared our stories of how God answered our prayers. The more we shared, the more they wanted to hear, saying, "tell us some more stories. When we grow old, we want to be like you."

That evening, on Jerusalem's streets, the group sang to the crowds and spoke about their Messiah, Jesus. We enjoyed the atmosphere that night and, the next day travelled to Masada with them. A fascinating place that the Israelis hold deep within their hearts. Masada is a high mountain top where the Romans had attacked the Jews, and after a long siege, the Jews committed mass suicide to escape their tyranny. Only nine out of the nine thousand people escaped. "It will never happen again," they've promised themselves.

Meanwhile, it was delightful being around these lovely young people. They invited us to go with them to Bethlehem. After visiting the church of the nativity and their Lutheran church, we went for a "swim" in the Dead Sea. I then discovered the group was to visit Kenya next. "Oh, I have just come from there," I told them. On the bus trip back into Jerusalem, I taught them some Swahili. After only two weeks' stay in Kenya, you could imagine the lesson was pretty elementary.

We treasured our time in Jerusalem and revelled in the experience of walking along paths that Jesus had once walked. We worshipped in an Arminian church as well as with the Greek Orthodox and Ethiopian churches. We also attended services in a Pentecostal church and witnessed a Bar Mitzvah at a Messianic church. A simple and moving service in the Franciscan church was our favourite.

Beyond Jerusalem, we travelled by public transport to the north of Akko and worked in a nursing home for survivors of the holocaust. We were so moved by these Israelis who had finally returned to their homeland after experiencing so much horror. While up north, we attended a Palestinian Christian church that had an Egyptian prophet visiting. After the service, he prophesied over Robyn that she would have an international ministry. God told me many years later that the prophecy given to Robyn was correct but that it was meant for me.

Robyn was flying back to Australia from Tel Aviv, and I would be flying into Sydney from Amman in Jordon. To get to Jordan, I caught a bus from Bet Shan. After many hours, in the middle of nowhere, it suddenly stopped. The driver said to me, "Lady, this is where you get out. It is your exit point." I fumbled down the bus stairs, and my feet touched the burning sand. "A taxi would come along soon," he shouted as the door closed behind me. There, in the echoing stillness, I looked out as far as my eye could see. *I'm by myself in the middle of nowhere*, I thought. Dumped and sleeping in the desert that night- oh well.

The hot sun seared my skin, when suddenly, I heard a faint noise. In the distance, sure enough, a taxi speeding along, leaving a trail of dust. It stopped, picked me up and dropped me off at the nearby checkpoint, and then sped away.

An Israeli couple saw me wandering around by myself. "She is alone," the wife said, "let's see where she is going. Can we help you?" they asked. After a brief conversation, they kindly showed me exactly what I had to do, then offered to travel twenty-five kilometres with me in a shared taxi to Amman. At my hotel, they said their goodbyes, and as I closed my hotel door, it was with a thankful heart. My heavenly Father, who is always with me and very present in times of trouble, provided this couple to care for me.

Over the next few days in Jordon, the highlight of standing on Mount Nebo where Moses had stood when he viewed the promised Land was breathtaking. The following day, I flew back to Australia. It had been quite a year.

A flame they lit,

and my heart never the same

I had to follow and forget my game.

23

THE TUG

Back home, my heart was smitten. I saw a great need in Africa, and I couldn't wipe the smile off my face. I felt the tug towards going back, and I was hoping it was a sign. One day while praying, God overjoyed my spirit. "I have work for you to do there," He said. I jumped right in, and straightaway began a three-month course on "Perspectives." The study was intense yet very helpful in preparing my mind and heart for the foreign field. I stayed with friends overnight as the course was held in the evenings quite a distance from home.

Shortly afterward, I found myself chatting to a young church member about my interest in Africa and told her how I had been asked to develop a teaching module for the community development program. She replied with some very helpful information that put me in great stead for the future programs. During our discussion, it became clear to me that God was mapping out new paths for me to walk along. On a more complex level, these paths were unfamiliar and ones I had not trodden before, and in that sense, they held some darkness to them. Hunger leads to desire. I was hungry to know more about what God was doing with me.

God often said I was in a time of preparation and training. In many ways, the learning process had already begun for at the time our welfare program was having financial problems. Developing a strong faith for an outpouring of finances would be part of my training. God, being the gentle teacher that He is, began giving me visions and spiritual pictures that shed much light on my difficulties.

"You are in a spiritual battle," He said.

"You must be spiritually protected so you can disarm the dark spiritual powers trying to intimidate you."

"Spiritual forces are not as powerful as they might seem. At the Cross, I destroyed their ability to hurt, but you must speak to disarm their presence," God said. He then went on to teach me that when we come into agreement with Him about our situation, we activate divine power, "for our weapons of our warfare are not carnal but mighty in God for pulling down strongholds, casting down arguments and every high thing that exalts itself against the knowledge of God." 2 Corinthians 10:4-5 NKJ

In this way, the Bible becomes a sword able to cut through the obstacles, and His word also a key that opens the heavenly treasure chest.

He already could see the doubts and fears in my heart, and He knew what else was in there. God, our father, is compassionate towards our fears, and He always helps us see things from His abundant perspective. He then challenged me with this question, "Is anything too hard for Me? I own the cattle on a thousand hills, and everything is mine. With me, everything is possible."

I knew nothing was impossible. But there were parts of me in which I felt many things were, in fact, too hard. On earth, I could see that there were many needs, with money scarcely available. In that sense, I didn't feel everything belonged to God. Modern man today is very busy building empires of their own. Their tiny kingdoms. "To train my children into greatness," God said, "I keep the windows of heaven shut, for a shut-up heaven makes you curious." I could see what He meant, for the need does get our attention.

Yet, in many ways, I had two minds about prayer. God was ever so gently drawing me in with the visions He gave me, and in that sense, I knew He had all the answers. But in another sense, I was highly distracted by the amount of work that lay before me. The pioneer in me would be dreaming of transformations and how it could all be achieved, and I never had time to stop and hear just in case God didn't like my ideas.

A little while after this, in a vision, I saw myself driving a car with Jesus in the passenger seat. He said to me, "Let me drive." So, we were about to change over, but I wouldn't let go of the steering wheel; I was gripping it so tightly you could see the whites of my knuckles. So, he had to unfurl my fingers gently one by one before He could take the wheel. As a passenger, I said, "I know a terrific shortcut." He then said, "I am the driver, I know the way we are going. There is danger down there that you are not aware of." I knew God was asking me to allow Him to set the direction for my life.

***

During our weekly catchups with my friends, I appeared very settled in Australia, but my heart was in Africa. When my heart is happy, it does cartwheels, and that's what it was doing when I met Florence. She lives in Kenya and was in Australia visiting her son and his family. We exchanged details, and I carefully put her phone number inside my backpack for when I was next abroad.

Next abroad wasn't too far off, for, in October, I threw some more things in my little backpack and shut the front door behind me. I arrived in Nairobi to the news that Pastor Harold and Ruth were remaining in England, and I would be here by myself for the very first time. He did arrange for me to be picked up at the airport and taken to stay overnight at Bishop Simon's place. I needed to catch a bus to Kitale the next day, and Bishop Simon's daughter drove me to the bus station. We were running late, but she wasn't fazed; she just mounted the pavement and drove on it to avoid the traffic. I was horrified, but I got to the bus stop with a few minutes to spare. There, on the front seat of the old coach for the next seven hours, I enjoyed a comfortable ride to Kitale.

It was already evening when the bus dropped me off. No sooner had I opened the front door and stepped inside when the lights suddenly went out. I tried adjusting my eyes to the deep darkness, and not knowing where the torch or candles were, I fumbled around for what seemed hours trying to organise my luggage. *Welcome to Kenya Marie!* I thought to myself.

The following day, I awoke to a tiny postage stamp garden outside my front door and beyond that, dirt roads and a big rambling house high on the hill. I later learned that the row of small flats I was staying in was owned by the person who lived in that house.

While in Kitale, I would be living by myself in Pastor Harold's flat- the one he rented off the man on the hill. The best thing about the little two-bedroom flat was the huge shower in the bathroom, and it was the first thing I found when the lights came back on last night. As the sun shone into the tiny kitchen this morning, I put on the kettle and settled in for a nice hot cup of tea.

The compound was stark bare, much like a new housing estate that had not yet planted trees or developed the site. Later in the week, I walked three kilometres into the town. It's something I would do regularly. On those dusty roads, I'd pass women cleverly carrying piles of wood on their heads and be aware of the thrill that finally, I was where my heart wanted me to be.

Kitale had a real African feel, numerous supermarkets and brightly painted shops cradled by various wide, dusty roads. Africa was like this; sprawling western-like towns and cities.

Surrounding Kitale were some impoverished and run-down villages that only had one water tap and lots of chooks running around. It was these villages reeking with poverty that pulled on my heartstrings.

Motorbikes, pushbikes, matatus- the choices of taxis were endless. After finishing the shopping, I would hop on the back of a motorbike and relish the wind sweeping my hair as we sped along. Further up the hill, I could see my compound where I had all my things. Usually, the taxi would stop at the gate, but he rode straight on through for the security guard was at lunch.

Living by myself in the flat was enjoyable until, of course, the blackouts had me sitting at night in the pitch-black, sometimes in the middle of dinner, other times, while reading. Due to the frequent reoccurrences, I kept a candle close by and always carried a torch.

Close by were two orphanages. In one of them, Rosemary was caring for fifteen children. She lived up around the corner, and was a school teacher. She and her late husband had started the orphanage, and after he died, she continued on herself. Margot and I decided to sponsor her children as she did an excellent job with them.

The other one was run by the Elim Church, but the children from there heard about this white lady, found out where I lived and came knocking on my door. Children always make me feel young at heart and I love their innocence towards life. In no time, lots of boys and girls were all cramming inside my flat. They didn't come for a quick visit, they wanted to get to know me. So, I had a great time teaching the boys how to play simple games such as noughts and crosses and hangman- played with one piece of paper and a pencil. I taught the girls how to make pancakes. I and they, enjoyed the visits.

Then, a highlight of the year was the agricultural show. I took twelve of the children, and some rode a camel; others went on the merry-go-round. They had chips and ice cream for lunch, and each one was given $1.00 to spend. How much fun they had in deciding what to spend that money on.

Rosemary taught me Swahili for the princely sum of $3.00 each week. To increase my vocabulary, I faithfully did my Swahili homework each week and practiced wherever I could. I often travelled on the local matatu, a twelve-seater minibus usually packed to capacity with the conductor hanging precariously onto the outside of the door of the vehicle. I never once saw another mzungu (white person) traveling on a matatu, but I loved them because they were a good way of meeting people and practicing my Swahili.

One day, I was on the bus, silently studying my little Swahili book when an old man sitting beside me snatched it out of my hand and said, "I will be your teacher." He proceeded to ask me questions. Every time I got something wrong, he would very sternly say, "No, NO, No!" The atmosphere in the bus began filling with quiet giggles until it finished in an uproar of laughter.

While I could speak some Swahili, I always used an interpreter when teaching. African houses typically are made from mud, have no windows, but usually an iron roof, and a kitchen outside. In one such house, I shared with a small group of women some personal experiences on how God helped me over the years and how He had healed my marriage. Many of those going through difficulties and problems in their own homes felt both supported and encouraged.

I had previously met an Elim pastor on my first visit to Africa with Margot. Back then, he had invited me to teach seventy of his high school students at his church. He was also the Abundant Waters Bible School dean and invited me to work with him there. This pastor would become a stragegic part of God's purposes in the future.

Back home, our discipleship training course had been a great success, and I now felt it essential new Christians in Kenya had a deep connection with God so that they were ready to face whatever came their way to discourage them. So, I began teaching from those same discipleship training manual. The young Kenyans learnt to stand against the wiles of the devil through a strong level of faith. Several were incredibly blessed. When God first asked me to teach some years ago, I said, "I am willing to do this, but I cannot do this afraid. Please, you will have to take away all fear of speaking in public." From that day on, I have only felt peace and confidence.

God is so gracious to meet us in our weaknesses. We taught Bible stories to fifteen kids in a two tiny roomed school situated in his compound. His wife ran the school.

I was never short of friends. It was easy getting to know the locals as many of them were very welcoming to me. There was a particular businesswoman whose chauffeur was ripping her off. I offered to teach her to drive so she could take herself to her meetings.

In our first lesson she drove her massive car on a very narrow dirt road when I saw a wide bus heading straight for us. I said to her, "Stop and let him drive past you. He knows what to do." But she pulled right over instead, and as she did, the car began sliding into a six-foot ditch, and the back wheels were dangling over it. "Help Lord," we cried. We did not know what to do. Suddenly, six strong Kenyan men came out from nowhere, picked that huge car up, and put it back on the road. Another day out driving, we saw thirty baboons cross the road in front of us. It was so amazing to see as I felt I was in some foreign film. We called into a roadside café, and she taught me how to eat ugali and mboga with my hands - their tradition. I was happy to be becoming more immersed in the culture.

Then when Helen came to my door selling beautifully coloured roses for $2 a bunch, I invited her in for a chat. I wanted to support her as she was trying so hard to make a living. She often joined me for lunch, and we had good discussions together, and we became great friends. One day I asked her to show me how to carry the basket on my head as she did. The results were hilarious as I wobbled from side to side.

Now and then, in these preliminary days, I questioned myself as to why I was in Kenya and whether or not it was God's will. At dinner one night, I overheard a reputable person say, "oh, what shall we do with that old lady?" I thought to myself, *yes, what will you do*! I asked God for confirmation as to whether He wanted me there, and he said, "I will make you a light to the Gentiles that you may bring my salvation to the ends of the earth." I knew for sure that God had a plan for me, and He would unfold it in His time. But I was impatient even though I had a lot to be encouraged by.

I was undoubtedly encouraged when I visited the school in Rafiki village where the feeding program was in progress. The principal was delighted my sister and I had started it, for not only were there no more fainting from hunger, the children were much more attentive in class, and the enrolments at the school had increased substantially. This is the sort of change that results from one or two people putting their hand up and saying *yes, I can help*.

While it was a lot of fun living with the locals and being part of their lives, it was sometimes easy to feel isolated. When I was so far from loved ones at home, I realised my family held me in their hearts, and it mattered I was so isolated from everything familiar. An unexpected phone call from Margot assuring me of her prayers meant the world to me. Then news had reached my boys in Australia that I had become sick with malaria. "I am coming to bring you home," said Frazer.

"I am in good hands here," I retorted. But were they convinced?

24

SAFARI

Frazer was not convinced, for he was on the verge of flying to Kenya to take me home. It really did take quite a bit to convince them I was in good hands. During my recovery, I felt exhausted and needed a break to enjoy some relaxation. I decided to go to Nakuru for a short safari. My next-door neighbours were happy to come along also, and together we took the four-hour drive there. We stayed overnight, some in tents, but there was a youth hostel in the national park, so I stayed in that. Early next morning, in an open-top jeep, we began a six-hour drive around the park.

The following morning, at 5 am, we were again warned of the dangers of standing in the open-top jeep and were asked to focus straight ahead and keep a firm hold on the railings. But this sort of warning was hard to adhere to when roaming African animals are everywhere, and trees are full of fascinating birds.

Distracted, I forgot the instructions, and suddenly, when I was neither holding on nor concentrating, the driver abruptly slammed on the brakes. I nearly flew over into the lap of a massive python about four metres long, slithering across the road. This incident marked the end of two refreshing exhilarating days.

On my return, Pastor Harold and Ruth arrived in from England. I was so pleased to see them as it had often been quite a challenge on my own. The following day, we visited Florence. She is one of the many outstanding women in Africa who have hearts that think beyond themselves and know how to make something out of nothing. Florence was more than the average woman, and during our visit, we learned she had trained widows in agriculture and taught them to care for orphans from those gardens. She also lobbied to get a high school built in her village.

I had been working on the module for the community development, but pastor Harold said he wasn't ready for it to be taught yet. I was invited to teach it at another venue, and Ruth was there listening to me. She later said, "Marie, you are a born teacher."

In these early days, not every project we started was successful. In one instance, I just steamed ahead without direction from God. It seemed an excellent plan to create a project leasing a large block of land to cultivate by ten families in the church. The project was successful, but the coordinator ran off with all the money, and the project collapsed. The lesson was learned. In the future, we needed to engage with the right people who understood business principles. Imposing my solutions from the outside was never going to work, and I was on a steep learning curve.

In a nearby village, we helped provide shoes for three little bare-footed girls who had been attacked by jiggers and had become partially paralysed. It was shocking to see.

To many Kenyans, a mud hut with two beds and a chair is luxury. In typical African hospitality, Mary enjoyed this luxury and opened her tiny home up for a women's fellowship group. Ruth and I were invited, and we all crammed into the room. I sat on the bed and others on the floor, and we all sang together and prayed. Mary brought some hot tea in for us all made in her open-fire kitchen outside. I felt so at home. These were my brothers and sisters, and I felt a real kinship with them. I shared that I was a pleasure seeker in my younger days but found it an empty life until I found Jesus.

Ruth shared from Nehemiah. When it was time to leave, it had been raining heavily, and the driveway was very slippery. While reversing, Ruth hit a pole and scraped the side of the vehicle, and became bogged. Out of nowhere, ten strapping men became mud-covered from head to toe, trying to push us out.

A few days later, Pastor Harold and Ruth drove me to Nairobi, a seven-hour journey, and I stayed overnight at the bishop's house. At the airport, I said a fond farewell and climbed aboard the plane bound for Australia.

It was so good to see my family again at Christmas, and we had an exceptional celebration together. Graham and Wendy spent Christmas Eve with me, and very early on Christmas morning, we all flew to Melbourne to holiday with Mark and his family. We had a lovely family time together watching India play Australia in the test match at the Melbourne Cricket Ground. My family are mad-keen cricketers, so that especially was wonderful. We also went to Werribee Open Plains Zoo, and the kids just loved seeing all the animals. It was great to see the four cousins enjoying each other's company.

2012

After the Christmas break, things took a very unexpected turn when our office at Claymore was torched by fire. They say not everything lasts forever, and the next few weeks proved to be a new beginning for me. At our new office in Airds, after two separate significant errors in my counselling sessions, I was not needed for the next three weeks. It was a shock and something I do with all the blows in my life - I took it to the Lord in prayer.

"Lord, are you telling me that my time with the community services is finishing?"

After some lengthy discussion with God in prayer, I felt that was indeed what He was saying. For ten years, God had been training me. I had many experiences, and I had learned a lot in helping the poverty-stricken here in Australia. With that door now closing, God redirected me to the needs of the people in poverty-stricken Africa.

My time was freed up to concentrate my efforts on Africa. I began working on the teaching module. Then at church, I was encouraged, when, during prayer, my favourite pastor saw me as an overloaded apple tree, and many were catching ripened fruit from me. Another prophesied that I was entering a period of increased influence, and I'd be a robust and steady pillar of support in the church. As I walked into the unknown years ahead of me in Africa, these insightful words became a light to my path and water to my thirsty soul.

The year passed quickly, and I boarded a plane to Nairobi via Paris and onto England. In Paris, I met a wonderful American harpist studying French history, and she generously took me to see the Chateau Fontainebleau, Napoleon's favourite residence. We ended a magical day with the locals in the town square dining on *Pate de fois gras* and strawberry tartlets – Magnifique!

Graham and his family were in town with me and other family members all getting ready for Frazer and Lisa's wedding in London. Two days prior, Frazer's fiancé, who works at the Lawn Tennis Association, gifted all of us tickets to Wimbledon. What a treat!

The couple's special day dawned perfectly. Just like his dad, Frazer is an adventurous soul and very unconventional and his wedding day was no exception. The bride and groom organised a rather out of the ordinary ceremony in a barn sporting Jewish and African traditions. Everyone, including the bride and groom were dressed in country and western-style clothes.

It was a wonderfully relaxing day, full of fun and laughter and we all enjoyed the informality. It was hilarious to watch the many games afterward in the farmyard. I was so happy to see my youngest son married that day.

25

LOCAL NEEDS

A bit of glamour and fanciness is something I enjoy when abroad. My sisters and their families joined me at Sharrow Bay in the Lakes District for a sumptuous afternoon tea. I mean the sort a palace would boast. Its other claim to fame - Paul McCartney and Heather Mills became engaged there.

Back in London, I was just finishing a historic walk when the guide pointed to a church in the distance and said, "John Newton was the minister at that church." It was lunchtime, and ecstatic at the thought of visiting it, I walked into its Pentecostal meeting. Like a cool breeze on a hot summer's day, the melodic sounds of the praise and worship washed over me. Utterly refreshed by worship, I then spoke to the vicar and told him of my work in Kenya, and he happily prayed for me. I thought it was God's seal, and my heart was bursting with joy and excitement for the task that lay ahead.

Then it happened, the roaring sound of touch down at Nairobi airport. Now, I was for the third time in Kenya, and having worked on the Community Development course, I was excited to teach it for the very first time. The poverty was palpable at Mois Bridge. Over crowded streets, a bit much like a football grand final with people aimlessly wandering, some more intentional and pop-up stands selling street food and rattling trucks and kids waiting in groups for their parents to return.

The inaugural class was held at a Bible school where seventy pastors from surrounding villages were on their way to becoming financially independent. Sometimes, in most poverty- stricken villages, it is hard to articulate beyond the obvious need for water, food, shelter, shoes, and clothing. But these pastors were already dreaming beyond attaining those basics needs. Instead of relying on overseas aid, they learnt to identify their specific needs in each of their villages and then find those in their community who might have the skills, knowledge, and resources to meet those needs. Each village then organised community banking and by collaborating, they set up small businesses. The locals could see the sense in this program. They enjoyed the idea of identifying their own skills that would lift them from poverty. I had a dream about this program, it was a secret that I kept stictly to myself- hidden deep within my heart, yet to be revealed later on in one of the chapters.

When I wasn't teaching, I was alone in my tiny flat a lot of the time. With no television, I'd regularly go to the local Christian bookshop, come back with an arm full of biographies, and spend many happy hours buried in their pages. At the time, a federal election was imminent. Previously, during such elections tribal violence had erupted and many lives were lost. This election looked less promising. I happened to be reading *John Wesley- A Biography* and his rendition of the best way to hold an election in it. They were to (1) vote for the person they judged most worthy. (2) To speak no evil of the opposition and (3) to take care, their spirits weren't sharpened against those who voted for the other side (Tomkins, 2003).

These principles seemed so very relevant for this current situation. Even though I wanted to influence it positively, a wide distribution of this information was beyond me. So, I prayed about it and left it in God's hands.

My three-month stay in Kenya had ended, and my journey home began with a trip back to Nairobi. The day before my departure, I was staying at Bishop Simon's house and was delighted to meet a christian politician who was visiting at this time. I felt that he was the very person to circulate John Wesley's three principles. He listened intently and promised he would see to it. In the election that followed, there was no tribal violence and no injuries. Our God "is able to do exceedingly abundantly above all we ask or think." Ephesians 3:20 NKJ

2013

Meanwhile, Darren and Claire, a couple from my church asked God about His will for their lives. To each one, He separately said, "go and talk with Marie." Over dinner, I told them about my trips to Kenya, and most enthusiastically, they responded. "We are resourceful and can build or do anything else you'd like; we would like to join you next time." I drove home that night full of excitement. A committee was set up shortly afterward to support the work, and Darren and Claire became foundation members.

Africa was becoming a significant focus, and I always looked forward to my return there. In June, again, happily I packed my backpack for the weather in both England and Africa. During the usual stopover in England, I experienced the joys of seeing family again and revelled in all London offers, including the pageantry at Buckingham Palace.

I was on my way to Kenya and at Nairobi airport was met by Pastor Harold. A little later in the week, he, Ruth, and I travelled through the magnificent green countryside of the Great Rift Valley, enjoying the wide-open skies and colour dotting villages. My trips through the African countryside were never boring and always full of new things to see.

The very enthusiastic Elim Pastor was waiting for me at Kitale. He was interested in both our programs and over the next six weeks, had eighty-five teenagers at his church waiting for me on Sunday mornings to teach them the discipleship program. They were from a local Christian school, and by the second week, about twenty students came forward for prayer; many were filled with the Holy Spirit, and healings and miracles occurred.

Within a few days of arriving in Kitale, Pastor Harold was rushed to hospital with breathing problems. He needed to return to England for treatment. Everyone was so sad for wherever he went, he was universally loved. He had to be one of the most exemplary Christians I have ever met.

A Game Changer – the twist.

The students from Mois Bridge, who attended the first ever Community Development course were about to graduate. To celebrate, I decided to present their certificates at a formal ceremony. Knowing about African time, I handed out a questionnaire while I was waiting for the ceremony to start. I wanted to find out what they had done with the training, whether they began the projects, improved on their plans and how their families and communities had been impacted. When the questionnaires were returned, I was stunned to read that each village had done something different.

"We have started chicken farms, and we are raising goats, pigs, sheep, rabbit, and fish. We are growing vegetables. We have a welding business, brick-making business, tailoring shop, a hairdresser shop, and even a driving school for motorbike drivers." They had done all of this using the eight-hour teaching given them the previous year. They had formed groups with very little money and started saving and set up income-producing businesses, just as they had been taught.

My first reaction was, "Oh, are they telling me the truth?" So, I organised for an independent survey team to go and visit the twenty villages. They came back and told me, "They are not at all exaggerating, and we found them faithfully doing as they had said."

I then asked the students, "Well, how can we help you?" They did not ask for financial assistance but instead asked for practical skills training.

"We need to know how to prevent the chickens from dying or what to do in the dry seasons with the vegetables."

I only intended to present certificates to the graduating students, but when I saw the results- immediately, I realised the training had significant ramifications for these beautiful people.

So, we set up a training unit. The Elim pastor was knowledgeable and highly intelligent and not only was he in charge of a church and dean of a bible school, but now had another job. He was appointed the coordinator and organised all the training activities. We named the pilot program "Community training and empowerment," COMMUTREM for short. Each month, the coordinator would ask the people, "What are your needs, issues, or problems?" Depending on their answers, he would then go to the Department of Agriculture and get an expert to come out and answer their questions. From then on, the various experts came to the training days. This made the training days enormously successful, and at one time attracted as many as two hundred and seventy people. I was so excited to see what God was doing, and it was such a privilege to be part of it. Yet God often told me that I was not his first choice for this massive project. He said, "Nor are you the one most qualified to do this, but you are the one who put your hand up and said yes with a willing heart."

I was so glad I had responded.

26

MIRACLES

Life was full in Kitale, but it wasn't always easy in this beautiful town doing its best to become more westernised. What with almost daily power cuts, and at one stage, I was desperate for a shower after five days of no water. So, I knocked on the door of an American couple who I had only met once. With no need to plead, they gladly showed me their bathroom. Then we heard news that terrorists had taken over a major shopping mall in Nairobi. Although eight hours from here, I had not long been there, and it is my second home in Africa. In Nairobi, nine people were killed, and many were held hostage. The following day, the shopping mall was blown up, and many more were injured and even died. Situations like this often had my family extremely worried about me, and I assured them that I was not in Nairobi at the time of the attack. Instead, I had come to Kitale, three hundred kilometres further on.

The locals in Kitale were good-natured, and I made many friends there. But Elizabeth and Elsa, who lived nearby, were more than just casual friends. They became my dearest and closest friends. Elizabeth taught at a bible school, and together we went to a tiny village church every Sunday, where she often preached. Elsa also walked very close to God. She told me that she had been working in refugee camps and part of her role was to distribute blankets to the refugees. The Christians said, "don't give them to the Muslims, and only give them to the Christians."

"No way," she retorted. "God loves everybody." A few weeks later, Elsa spoke to a ninety-year-old witch doctor in Kenya, and consequently, he was converted to Jesus. This man had many politicians consulting him, and his salvation caused a great stir, and two men were sent to kill Elsa. They came knocking on her door and said, "We want to see Elsa."

"I am Elsa," she said.

"You, you're the one who gave us the blankets in the refugee camp; we can't kill you!" and with that, they left.

Elsa had many other stories like this. It was as if she had just stepped out of the book of Acts. I loved both her and Elizabeth, and learned so much from their close relationship with God.

Enroute to the airport, I stopped overnight at Nairobi, where Bishop Martin had taken the opportunity to glean the last drop of teaching from me before my flight. Unbeknown to me, he organised a spur-of-the-moment meeting, and it became a class full of volunteer tutors from Haapnet. At the end of that teaching, I thought to myself, *what a waste of time; they will never do anything with that teaching.*

How wrong I was. Bishop Martin and his wife Lydia lived in a slum area to minister to the poor and support them. After their training, over the next few months, in Bishop Martin's two room house, Lydia set up classes and taught thirty unemployed women and youth. Sewing in one corner, jewellery making in another, and knitting and leatherwork in the other corners. Eventually thirty businesses were established and the slum changed dramatically. Bishop Steve and his wife Chloe were also in that community development class. He was so impressed by the teaching that began raising pigs to sell and, as well, he also became a teacher for the program, travelling to many different countries. He and his wife, to help mothers who worked, set up a preschool.

Many of my newfound friends came to see me off at the airport, and I was sad about saying goodbye. As the plane sat on the runway, gearing up ready for take off, I mulled over in my mind all that God had done over the last year.

Tribalism had decreased in many villages and further to this, hundreds of people were now finding a greater purpose in using their skills. Parents were also able to feed their children and the hope of a promising future lay before them. Many young people had been strengthened in their faith through the discipleship program. Many were now tithing, and this meant that some villages even were able to help the widows and orphans and build new churches.

I saw the hand of God over all of this. I was just so glad that in my mid-seventies, I had said Yes to God and I was so grateful that He allowed me to be a part of His plan to eradicate poverty in Africa. This was only the start, and there was so much more to come!

2014

Back in Australia, at the annual C3 international conference, Pastor Brian Houston from Hillsong preached on "believing the secrets that God has placed in your heart." As I listened, I thought back to the secret that I had tucked away in my heart. It was so enormous – I had to make sure only God and I knew about it.

The more I treasured this idea, the deeper it was put out of sight. For even I found it hard to believe the community development teaching would go worldwide.

Over time, the more I came to believe God would make way for it to become possible, the more probable it became to me. The dream that was in me meant that I had to be sure of God's continual and total protection over my life. Shortly after the conference, I was driving on a rain-drenched road through the Royal National Park on my way to my sons' place. Rounding a corner, I went into a significant skid on the slippery surface. The wheels stopped just short of a ditch on the other side of the road. I wrenched the steering wheel around, which got me back onto the right side of the road. A few seconds later, three cars sped around the corner and could have caused a major crash. I was shaken up but very aware of God's protection.

It was becoming such an adventure to sit before God in prayer and listen to what He has to say. I never know what I will hear or see – one particular time, I saw a picture of a river meandering slowly through pleasant fields of flowers. Then I saw a brook that was joyfully tumbling over rocks intent on getting to its destination.

"So, what's this about," I asked Jesus. He said, "We have two courses. We can choose to meander and life would be pleasant but not much is attempted and not much achieved. This river is life without purpose, but the brook babbles purposefully along. It goes directly to its destination." That day, I learnt from this analogy that my life's course and direction would flow from my attitudes towards God's Word. I wanted to choose life with purpose by obedience and belief in God's promises and was so glad that God challenged me to believe for great things at my late stage of life. He would often remind me, "You can pray for big things or small things. The choice is yours, but I am a big God." Praying for the impossible seemed a challenge, but even so, I was up for that. So, I chose to believe for answers to big prayers.

Shortly afterward, the miracles started jumping up in front of me. God told a young couple from a nearby Church to give the spare money they were praying about to me. When they handed me the envelope with the $1,000, I was so encouraged - that my God indeed was the *God of the impossible.*

I kept following upwards as I followed along

My questioning heart

became very strong

27

THE BUS SEAT

Mostly always, answers to my prayers turn into a sort of an adventure where I would be given my heart's desire.

Darren and Claire arrived in Kenya with me on the 3rd of September. We straightaway caught a bus to Kitale. It was a new adventure for my friends, and they soaked up every minute. All the while, I was sitting on another seat, on the lookout for new contacts to become part of this program.

"Excuse me, lady, you are sitting on my seat." I looked up to see a man with the broadest smile looking down upon me."

"Oh, I don't think so," I replied.

We both checked our tickets and with nothing more said, and the man sat down, happy to have sorted his query.

"Hello." The man introduced himself as Situma from Kenya.

"So why are you here," he asked. His lovely posture and gentle tone had already set me at ease and I felt very comfortable. "Well," I said, "it all started a few years ago. My sister's pastor invited her and me to visit him in Kitale. He took us to a village where our hearts were broken by the poverty there." Over the next five hours, I told him everything. He sat intently listening, and I could see his ears prick up as I told him the impact the community development program was having. He was leaning in towards me *and becoming very interested.* I could feel the excitement growing in me and in him too.

Situma went on to tell me that he had an international

business in change management. Previously, also he had worked for the United Nations and the World Bank. It soon became apparent he was a man of wisdom and knowledge, and one I desperately needed gleaning from. I told him of my immediate challenge on this trip was the prospect of rewriting the policies and procedures. It had been thirty years since I had worked on such things.

I asked if I could call him if I ran into any trouble, to which he gave me his phone number. By this time, my heart was doing triple somersaults. It indeed was a most wonderful experience sitting next to him on that bus seat especially that I was sitting beside a miracle and my next surprising adventure.

Darren, Claire and I arrived and I unlocked the silver door in the third flat along. All the apartments had silver doors, and often I would be struggling to open a door only to find it wasn't mine. The tiny garden was still blooming, and the grass at the top of the hill was still green. Looking out and seeing the wooden fence built around the entire compound was such a comfort to me. "It's to make the neighbourhood safer," a neighbour commented later that week.

Later that week, I met up with Situma. Over a cool lemonade, he offered to become my mentor and, right there, became the miracle I needed. He began teaching me many things. Over the following months, he developed an operational manual for us, plus a constitution, a strategic plan, and a sustainability plan. He told me he believed in what we were doing and charged us $300, 1/20 of his regular fee.

Our Kenyan coordinator was flourishing and enjoyed being deeply involved in Commutrem. He was keen to show Darren and Claire and me the new lives people were building for themselves. We visited the various villages where the community projects were in action. The road to our first stopover village was deeply potholed, nonetheless it took us to a vibrant community of happy people all wanting to support each other.

We were utterly amazed at this friendly, relaxed atmosphere in Mukunga, where we met Charles. He had built an organic garden, created a fish pond to farm fish, hired some land to raise sheep and cows, chickens and quail. He tried to convince me quail have significant health benefits, especially for older people. I took the egg and swallowed it and promised myself never to allow anyone to talk me into swallowing such things again.

Rosemary, an original student, lived further up the road at Matunda village. She was a visionary and planned to have at least ten projects by the time I visited her next. I heard how she exceeded those expectations, and we were keen to see the projects as we walked further along the dusty red ground. We were taken to a chicken farm and fruit and vegetable stores, a clothes shop, a school, a snack bar, a brickmaking business, and a tailoring and hairdressing shop.

These businesses lightened the load that poverty had caused and created a healthier community. The two ladies who ran the grain store told me,

"The teaching not only is benefitting us. See the motorbike drivers over there; they carry all our goods for us. The farmers are growing the staples for us to sell."

I was impressed with this chain reaction.

A beggar who set up a chicken farm said she had meat to eat and eggs to sell. When her chickens got into the neighbour's vegetable patch and caused problems, the pastor, a gifted communicator, another original student, was available to resolve the problem. He made himself available to help sort other problems common to groups of people forming a business and creating a cooperative to market their goods. It was an excellent opportunity to minister to the lives of many villagers.

Then at Mois Bridge, things had changed dramatically from when I first visited. Some of the poverty first seen began disappearing, and in its place, brick-making and pig farms. "Your teaching has changed our communities and has given us much hope," we were told.

We finished up at Kap- Koi, where they had started a school and were busy building a pig farm and making bricks.

Darrin and Claire spent a bit of time in Rafiki village building a kitchen to replace the old tin shed used to cook breakfast for the children. Darrin also ran a prophetic seminar, and the money I had received before I left for Africa was now something we were praying about. Darren and Claire felt that the $1,000 would be best spent buying a piki-piki (motorbike) for the Kenyan co-ordinator to travel around while visiting his various projects in remote areas. And so it was, the piki-piki was wheeled down the aisle at the Sunday morning service with much acclaim, and Darrin and Claire presented it to him.

Thankful for their adventures with me, Darren and Claire said their goodbyes and returned to Australia. They had gone home, and I was on my own.

Shortly afterwards, Rose arrived and stayed with me. I met Rose at my church. She had grown up in Zimbabwe and told me a fantastic story of angels protecting her property during the troubles in the 1970s. The farm that she had grown up on was attacked but she later learned that the attackers couldn't get past the perimeter fence because a row of gigantic men were defending it, and the attackers turned tail and fled. Being a woman of great faith, I enjoyed her company, and now she was in Africa with me.

Being friends, we had a lot of fun together. I learnt how she weaved a class on patchwork with the local ladies into lessons on prayer. "Life and prayer have to be stitched together often even daily," she tells the class. In various places, she used her skills to teach marketing for Haapnet and Commutrem and her wisdom to teach relationships. Rose and I travelled to Nyaharuru to do some teaching there. It was an arduous eight-hour trip, and just when I thought I could not endure sitting in one spot for another moment, the driver drove into a prominently large commercial town with many supermarkets and banks and further out, the famous Thompson Waterfall. The class was waiting, and I promptly began teaching. My interpreter was a beautiful young girl who had converted out of Islam and was cast out by her family. Many people pay a high price for becoming Christians in many developing countries. I liked having an interpreter as it allowed the extra time to think more clearly about what I wanted to say.

Every time we made an advance, there was an upheaval of some sort. We had a successful time at Nyaharuru, and after two days of showing the locals how to stand firm in their faith, the pain in my back was getting worse. We were scheduled to travel to Voi, another eight-hour trip. With the excruciating pain now worsening, I was seriously reconsidering whether I should not go on any further.

Rose and I prayed about it, and I felt God say, "Going on their way, they were healed." That settled the matter. On our journey, Rose became extremely sick, and we had to go to the hospital, and she was put on a rehydrating drip. It was apparent that we were under attack from the devil, and we were a threat to the work being furthered in Africa. Yet, even so, God had already got us covered because He said that *on their way, they would be healed*, and they meant both of us.

We arrived in Voi to one hundred bishops and pastors, all waiting and very keen to learn. News had reached them on how previously, the villages had been transformed. Now they wanted to take the teaching far and wide. After two days, the class formed themselves into table banking groups to save in view of starting their businesses.

On our return trip to Nairobi, we were driving through the

night and it was raining, in fact, lashing down. To make matters worse, we had taken a notoriously dangerous stretch of road where many people had been hijacked. "Stay out of sight," they told Rose and me. The night was incredibly dark, and the heavy rain caused the car to splutter and then stall to a halt. Bishop Martin opened the car bonnet, held a torch in his mouth, freeing his hands to find the problem. He then tried to stop passing vehicles, and after nearly despairing, a truck with a tow rope stopped and towed us to the nearest village ten kilometres away. It was 1.30 am when we finally pulled into a petrol garage. We all were so grateful to God for getting us safely there.

Rose had gone back to Australia, and I was now on my own in Kitale. It was only a five-minute walk, so I shut and bolted the silver door, and took myself off to the local pop-up stand selling food outside the hospital. I noticed a very well-dressed man roaming in the compound as I left. I assumed he was the real estate agent and didn't take too much notice. Then on coming back through the gate, I met a young man dressed in overalls, and again, I assumed he must be the workman I had been waiting on to fix the water. When I rounded the corner, I saw the padlock on the ground and my door wide open. The thieves had stolen my mobile phone, my binoculars, and the gas bottle. Fortunately, they did not find the considerable amount of money I had hidden.

A few days later Florence came to stay with me in Kitale. She was well-versed in community work, and it was important to me that she was impressed with the program and that it was culturally relevant to her. We went to church together and ate beef stew in a fancy little restaurant. It was such good fun having her with me. After this wonderful time with Florence, it was nearing the end of the year, and I was on my way home to Australia to celebrate Christmas with my boys and their families.

28

RESULTS

I had not missed an Agricultural Show in fifty years. In the evenings, the rodeos and fireworks were exciting, but my heart skipped a beat the next day when I saw a stall advertising a Christian microfinance charity. Intrigued, I took their brochure and, later that week, spoke with Ralf Schroers, the founder. He was very excited to be speaking to me and told me that he was looking for partners in Africa. After a brief conversation, he invited me to his office, and as I sat with him, I realised that he had been one of the top financial planners in Sydney. I discovered that *Microlend* also has the vision to end world poverty. Ralf told me that after his conversion, God told him to give his money to the poor. He instantly obeyed and sold his business and set up a Microfinance Charity. During our conversation, we agreed to work in partnership.

Florence and I had a lot in common, and we enjoyed each other's company. She was holidaying in Australia and stayed with me for a few days. I took her to my water aerobics class. She had never swum in a pool before but was keen to participate with the floating noodle, and I told her to just lay back on it and float. She did as she was told and promptly disappeared under the water with a flurry of splashes. There was great alarm, and many people quickly came to her aid. She resurfaced with a lot of coughing and spluttering. She was not too upset, though, and was happy to return the following week.

She told me how God had miraculously saved her from a freak car accident. I heard how she was near fatally pinned under the car in a swamp with only her nose and mouth and her eyes above water and one hand showing. During those horrific moments, the Lord ministered to her words of life. Some people came to help, but as they walked away from the wreck, thinking no one was there, they saw something moving, which they thought was a snake. On further inspection, they realised the snake was, in fact, a human hand. They frantically scrambled to set her free. She appeared lifeless and was taken to the local hospital and put in the morgue because they thought she was dead. After two hours, they came to remove her body, and someone said, "The body is still warm." They immediately began to resuscitate her, and within a few days, she was discharged from the hospital. What a testimony!

The end of June was bringing me up to our Golden wedding anniversary. I decided to return to the restaurant where Doug and I celebrated our long-life commitment to each other on our wedding night. Florence was still in Australia, so she and Robyn also came along. We took the ferry to *The Caprice,* one of Sydney's top waterfront restaurants. With a heart still aching over the man of my dreams, we nonetheless enjoyed the fabulous atmosphere. We ate lobster and an array of luscious desserts precisely as we had on our wedding night. Oh, the memories, and there on the balcony, overlooking the beautiful views of the harbour, I only wished Doug was with me.

I was in England again. Margot has an exquisite gift of sourcing low-priced entertainment and finding interesting places to see. This time while visiting, she had arranged for me to visit Kensington Palace. After lunch, I joined the talk on antiques and followed the exit sign back to the room where we had first assembled before lunch. On entering that room, now empty, the door shut behind me and locked itself. "Well, never mind, I will just go back," I thought.

So I turned to open the other of the two doors and found them to be locked also. I felt trapped and anxiously began to knock on the window, hoping to catch the eye of a passer-by. Eventually, a man saw me. "Help, I'm locked in," I mouthed. He hurried away and found a volunteer to set me free. The feeling of being locked in is never pleasant, but the adventurous spirit in me began to have visions of morning headlines the next day "intruder in the palace."

Each day, I was travelling back and forth into London, chasing up visas to get into Uganda, Tanzania, and Kenya. It was such a headache, especially when the final one took seven days. It was nerve-wracking. Finaly, it showed up at five in the afternoon the day before I was due to fly out.

Each time I return to Africa, of greatest interest, is the progress of the villagers and how they have improved their lives. When last I was at Voi, they had set up table banking and planned on saving to start their businesses. This training set them up to earn an income. So, when Bishop David told me they had bought two piki-piki bikes and a matatu to provide public transport, I was very excited. He also told me how they began a Childcare centre to make it easier for women to go out to work. He told me how even reluctant teenagers had been included in the program.

A young man who had been terrorising the neighbourhood had been so inspired by the teaching that he and two of his friends started a car washing business. The change in him was dramatic. Not only him but also other youth had their own businesses to get money. Stealing stopped, the crime rate went down and the overall security had significantly improved.

Another village changed almost overnight when a group of teenagers set up a rubbish removal business after identifing garbage as their biggest problem. The county governor was so pleased he funded a piece of equipment to help them in their work. This sort of news had my heart doing cartwheels. These stories inspired me so much so, I decided to travel with the bishops the long fifteen-hour drive to Tanzania.

We hadn't gone very far the following day when, on the outskirts of Nairobi, we became caught up in an episode of tribal violence. Large rocks and burning logs were on the road, and the piki-piki drivers were battling against the police, who, in return, were throwing tear gas into the rampaging mob and protecting themselves with shields and riot gear. We later learned the fighting was between the Masai tribe who had sold their land to the Kikuyu in Nairobi. This was many years ago when it was not worth much. Since then, Nairobi had grown, and the land was now valuable. The Masai people wanted it back and were retaliating. But the land rightly belonged to the Kikuyu tribe, and they refused to negotiate. Born into the Kikuyu tribe, Bishop Martin got out of the car and stepped into the firing line simply because he wanted to assess the situation. I was told afterward that he risk death at that point because he was a Kikuyu. Later I was informed that they had observed my reaction to the danger and were impressed by my calm composure and lack of fear.

Once past that dangerous bottleneck, the vast sprawling countryside opened up into a spectacular array of yellowy-green fields, sporting occasional zebras and antelopes. There were many Masai in traditional dress by the roadside and two young warriors painted black and white going through their year-long initiation period in which they must kill a lion with their bare hands.

We taught at the Babati Bible School. One morning during some quiet moments with God, I read about the vine. To explain this further, Jesus said to me that 'I am part of His tree, and that He is the root and I am the branch and that the power of the Holy Spirit (the sap) flows through me by faith.' I believed this truth, and literally could feel God's power flowing through me while I was giving this teaching.

In the next village, they refused to invite the entire community into the training, and they just wanted to keep it for their church members only, which usually fails.

Then, a little while later in Kenya, I climbed onto the back of the piki-piki and set off on the long journey to the middle of nowhere. We arrived at the place, and met up with one of our original students. His path to financial freedom started like this. After raising chickens, he sold them and bought cows, which he used to supply milk to all the local schools. He then brought a matatu to provide public transport. He had purchased a block of land adjacent his house, where he planned to build a new church.

The thing that thrilled me the most was when he said, "Tomorrow, I have one hundred and fifty women coming to the old church, and I am going to teach them what you taught me." To feed them all, he had a large sack of potatoes, and two sheep.

The ripple effect reached the entire district.

We then visited Samson, a young man who had been unemployed for five years. He went to a free organic farming course and started to farm a small block of land. Soon, he leased two other blocks of land and was joined by twenty-four young men. This transformation, going on before my very eyes, was incredibly inspiring.

I needed a break. So, I joined a three-day safari to the Masai Mara, the hightlight being the annual trek of two million wildebeest. Their journey began in Kenya, crossing the Mara River, reaching then the Serengeti in Tanzania. It had been my dream to see this, so for Mother's Day, my sons and their wives had gifted me with an opportunity to float above the Masai Mara in a hot air balloon. Watching the trek of wildebeest stretching out for hundreds of miles was breathtaking. From this height, I relished looking down on God's creation. This is how God sees us. Height is His perspective.

Back in Kitale, I was excited to visit the nearby newly formed C3 church. I was their first visitor from Australia and was invited to share my salvation testimony. As we sat on our plastic chairs under the shade of the sprawling avocado trees, they heard also of my call to Kenya. The congregation had grown to forty believers. Neighbouring Uganda now has the fastest-growing communities in the C3 movement, with over sixty new churches.

My outstanding memory of the trip to Uganda was teaching a group of young women who had babies with disabilities. I heard the heartbreaking story of a mother, whose child had hydrocephalus. She and all the others faced rejection when they returned to their families. The chaplain was trying to give them skills so that when they returned home, they could survive. God was opening doors. The needs were enormous. I sensed more and more that my whole life had been a preparation for the work in Africa.

To follow his footsteps and defend His heart is
the reason I began on this beautiful path.

29

WEEKLY DRINKS

It was such a joy to visit the local villages with traditional thatched huts and see all the projects. We were taken on a little tour and shown vegetable patches ready to be harvested. A young headman, Nathan, organised for the widows to share their stories of what God had done in their village.

I was thrilled to see that one of the widows was a Muslim, and it was evident that she felt accepted and at home within the group. We were shown Nathan's beekeeping project and were introduced to a man raising rabbits to sell. He was so proud of what he had achieved. Next, we were taken to see a vast nursery of trees and then shown a welding project and the plans someone had drawn up to build a greenhouse.

People were keen to tell us the transformation in their lives. Nathan had done an exceptional job at mobilising his community against poverty. Over and over again, I could just thank God for the privilege of allowing me to be part of what he was doing in Africa.

Each week I would meet for drinks with Situma. As we sipped our lemonade, I asked him questions, and he beautifully answered them. One day he said to me, "Marie, look, this teaching is so unique. I want to write a book about it with you." Later I discovered that he had written a publication in the Harvard University Library. His ability to influence local governors, write world-changing articles for universities, and chair numerous high-ranking meetings were impressive. Then, even more so, his humble, unassuming attitude was inspiring. I thanked God for bringing my life across his path.

On Sunday mornings, testimonies are a significant part of

the service, and being a mzungu (a foreigner), I am always invited to give mine. The people want to know if God is as real to me as He is to them. They tend to think that every mzungu is rich and does not need God to show up in their lives. I have a collection of testimonies, and their most favourite is how God supplied Doug with a pair of black shoes days before our wedding when we had no money. This always ministers to them, and they are always amazed to see that God supplies our needs in this way.

At the end of three wonderful months, the lemon-scented gum tree I would walk past every day was making me feel homesick. So, with that nostalgic feeling, I would take the leaves and crush them in my hand. The aroma took me back into my Australian backyard, and I found it very comforting. Before leaving Kenya, I had a rather longish meeting with Bishop Martin, and he told me Uganda, Tanzania, and Sudan were impressed and had invited us to take the program into their countries. God was opening doors, and we were beginning to see the fulfillment of the word given me all those years ago; the teaching would go into every developing country.

*****

2016

Back in Australia, my pastor challenged us all to ask God two questions. "What do you want to ask me, and what do you want from me."

In prayerful reflection to the second question, I felt God wanted me to give my finances to fund the program. I recalled God saying that my money was His and was to be spent as He guided. Easier said than done! Hudson Taylor never solicited funds. Even when his mission grew to over one thousand missionaries, he lived by faith and relied totally on God to supply all their needs. He continually challenged his readers to live a life of faith and often said, "God's work done in God's way, will never lack God's supply." I liked that. Especially the words 'never lack.'

I had always wanted to be living a great life - one that would get God's attention. I didn't want to be caught up in the ordinary sort of stuff...I had long finished with that. Time and time again, I read how generosity tugs at God's heart and makes one to be outstanding in his sight. I was being led one step at a time to use my own wealth to meet the needs in Africa. I hesitantly followed God's leading – and at the same time, God highlighted His promises for an abundant supply.

God was asking me to have more faith. He was telling me not to be anxious about the funding. Each time I agreed with God, he rewarded my faith. This time, a couple in the church donated $1,000 to the program, and the church itself gave $800.

I began treasuring these close encounters with God, it was precious that He kept allowing me to perceive what He was doing and saying to me. Instead of just praying and leaving my list on heaven's portal, I continued feeling deeply connected to my heavenly father.

At my church, a visiting pastor gladdened my heart during a time of prayer when I heard him say that God was planning on opening doors for me, and my hands would be used for healing, and He would increase the giving. My heart was happy now, for I felt God was affirming my place in Africa – and He was going on ahead to prepare the way.

Shortly afterward, with my backpack securely on my shoulders, I was again closing my front door. I arrived at Sydney airport to catch the 9.30 pm flight when my Airline announced that there had been a major crash in Dubai and they were not allowing planes to land there. An hour later, after they finished offloading the luggage, they reversed their decision. To beat the 11.00 pm curfew, they would have to fly out immediately and so could not reload. Even though the issue was adequately resolved with no harm at all done, I interpreted this chaos as a tremendous spiritual opposition to me going on this trip.

I am learning to believe in the promise that He who began this work will also bring it to completion. I pressed on in faith. Two days later, after arriving in England, Margot and I drove to Barnsley, where we did a self-guided tour on a Hudson Taylor trail. I have read countless times his two biographies, "Growth of a Soul" and "Growth of a Work of God." In my opinion, this is the best Christian biography ever written as it challenges us on almost every page to live a life of sacrifice. So, to be in the very spot where he grew up and where he first heard the call of God on his life was inspiring. Over the fifty years he faithfully ministered in China, Hudson Taylor saw thousands of Chinese come out of idolatry to trust in Christ. From those small beginnings, he saw that church grow into one of the largest in the world. The underground Christian church owes its origins to this fearless man of God.

From England, I was on my way to Kenya.

30

THE ALTAR

God's call upon our lives makes us unstoppable, and his energy and creativtiy rubs off on us (Williamson, 2011). God gave me a word of encouragement. "Enlarge the place of your tent, for you will spread out to the right and then to the left; you will not suffer shame." It was no time to retreat, and Bishop Martin confirmed this word by telling me he believed we should be reaching out to the rest of Africa.

In Zimbabwe, the teaching was very successful. Zimbabwe is a country of very high need. The President had been running the country into the ground by his excesses and extravagances. The pastors were so excited at the teaching and planned to put it into practice straight away.

The enthusiasm in one married couple was palpable when they came to see us one evening. The husband, in obedience to God's prompting, had given up his position as a lecturer in a prestigious Bible school in Wales and returned to his homeland in Africa to minister to the street kids. For a while now, he and his wife had been running a mission feeding and housing these orphans, teaching them the good news of salvation and sharing God's love. I was very impressed. We explained to this couple about the program's ability to help provide employment for the older teenagers. They then promptly went out and bought a block of land to teach them farming skills.

In Zambia, many told me how the teaching had utterly transformed their thinking and lives. It was heart-warming to see how enthusiastically it had been received and how many were keen to implement it. I travelled back to Kenya by Ethiopian airlines, arriving at Nairobi airport at 1.30 am. I found these early starts and late nights exhausting. Bishop

Martin and Bishop Steve did it a lot tougher as money was short. They spent three days travelling by bus to get back. I'm afraid that was just too much for me! On the teaching visits in Tanzania, Uganda, Zimbabwe, and Zambia, we saw that God was undoubtedly extending our borders, just as he promised. We had seen God working in people's lives to powerfully bring them the hope of a better future. They said the teaching had been received as a light. All over Africa, these lights were expelling the darkness poverty had caused and now bringing, instead, hope for a brighter future.

2017

In February, I received a very welcomed phone call from Bishop Martin, gladly telling me how he and his lovely wife are now devoting their lives to eradicating poverty worldwide. "My wife and I have put all on the altar," he said. It is the sort of thing one does when your life is dedicated to a grand vision. For me, it was such a comfort to be in partnership with these two beautiful souls and to have our lives knit together with one passion.

Both Bishop Martin and I have seen God's hand opening door after door and giving us favour in many countries. I have such great respect and admiration for this man – so gifted, yet so humble. His faith and enthusiasm know no bounds, and I consider it a great privilege to be working alongside him.

The following month God came to me and said, "Saturate your heart and soul in praise and worship." It seemed He knew the needs of the poor were consuming me and that I was working hard at poverty's eradication. He said that my strength would wane if I did not tap into His power. He said, "when your essence of becoming is connected to Me in worship, My power will flow through you, and My nature will be seen in you." Putting God first and doing his work in second place would mean a rearrangement of my priorities.

Towards the end of my seventies, I was conscious of the passage of time and felt the need for a long-term financial plan to be addressed. *Haapnet's* economic future was uncertain, and it was beginning to worry me. After discussing this with my pastor, I decided to make a will leaving it all to Haapnet. Many years before this, I had already given my three sons their inheritance after selling my house.

Shortly after this time, God insistently came to me yet again. I felt Him speak deep within my heart, "saturate yourself in My presence, worship Me in praise and adoration." I felt him telling me yet again that while world poverty was on his heart, I should prioritise a drawing closer to Him. Yet, it still didn't make sense. I could not understand how sitting and focusing on God would get the job done. Like, Martha of old, I have much to do, and I am a person of action. Constantly, throughout my journey, sitting hasn't been something I am good at doing...especially when in God's presence – for it is there, I become so inspired, and ideas come flooding into my mind on how I can help Him get the job done. I would often find myself running on ahead and, looking back, saying, "hurry up, Jesus, follow me."

I had been working very closely with Ralf from Microlend. His heart, made of gold, graciously provided finance for the extension of the local businesses connected with Commutrem. He was planning a trip to Nairobi, so I took the opportunity and asked if he would meet up with Bishop Martin and Archbishop Simon from Haapnet. He readily agreed to spend a few hours with them. Within minutes of arriving at Nairobi airport, his wallet and passport were stolen. The Australian embassy was closed for the weekend. There was little that could be immediately done at the time, so Bishop Martin promptly organised for him to teach business management to the tutors from Haapnet the following day. It was then agreed that he would fund Haapnet after he had finished with the other fundings.

Then Ralf arrived in Kitale and taught business plans and

management skills to one hundred aspiring business people from Commutrem. The students, who already had grown their businesses to saturation, applied for a loan to further develop their businesses. To show the extent to which the program was helping the locals, Ralf gave $80,000 to this flourishing program. To coordinate all this, Elsa became the new "in-house" microfinance manager. Elsa's new position encouraged me for it meant, yes, in fact, I would be able to hand the program over to the locals. The goal had been set. Within five years, it would become self-sufficient.

Elsa's new role as microfinance manager came to her in a sudden surprising manner. She had previously been in charge of an NGO, but someone had contacted the head office and told them many lies about her, and she had been stood down. When the Swedish benefactors came out to Africa to examine the problem, they quickly realised that it was not Elsa's fault and had promised to reinstate her with the next round of funding. Unfortunately, the Swedish government changed its policy on overseas funding, and the NGO was closed down.

When I was praying for Elsa, I saw a picture of her working as a waitress. She was standing next to a man at the head of the table, waiting to take his order. Although He had his back to me, I knew this man was Jesus. The table was laden with very basic food, nothing fancy, and one by one, the people were sitting down so they could be fed. Later this vision was fulfilled with her becoming the first microfinance manager for the pilot program.

Although Commutrem had been so successful, more and more, my heart was drawn to support Bishop Martin at Haapnet. He shared my vision and commitment to the poor. We rejoiced together as we saw God opening door after door in many countries. "We've had the Macedonian call," he would tell me excitedly as yet another country pleaded with us to take the teaching to them.

Work on the community development continued unhindered throughout the year. As we expanded into Uganda and Tanzania, it became apparent that we needed to source more funding. Our local federal M.P suggested we approach the Global Innovation Fund and promised to support the funding submission. However, there was still a lot of our in-house work needing attention. Our administrative structures needed addressing, and our policy and procedures required urgent attention.

31

A GOOD GOD

Commutrem was now becoming self-sufficient, and it was essential to examine how successful the program had been. We commissioned Situma to do an end-of-project evaluation.

The results were astounding. The teaching had reached 10,000 people and had transformed hundreds of communities. In one village alone, thirty different projects were currently running, and 1,200 people out of a population of 3,000 were involved. The evaluation identified that the program had been 80% successful, a result not reached by many other similar projects.

We discovered the United Nations had developed a sustainability plan for the world's growth with seventeen goals. I was very encouraged to learn that our community development program (CDP) objectives were the same as their first six goals; the eradication of world poverty, income and food security, health and education, and access to clean water.

Airport

I was on my way to Kenya again and stopped over in England. My sister and I travelled by train to Cornwall, we then upgraded the hire car. It was a rainy day with poor visibility, and I pulled out of a minor road right into the path of a black four-wheel drive. I just didn't see it! We escaped with only minor cuts and bruises. The upgrade proved to be a lifesaving decision as we were told that had it been a smaller car, we would have been killed outright. It was a shock, and I was greatly shaken. Everything in me interpreted this event as a spiritual battle- a form of opposition that I felt caught up in. I would soon learn that nothing in heaven or hell could stop God's hand from moving. I would know, not only in my mind but also deep within my heart, that greater is He within me than within the world. God protected me from significant harm.

After a lovely time with my family, I caught a plane from London to Malawi, where, exhausted, I lay on the airport seats and slept. I was still exhausted when I arrived and started the community development teaching the next day.

Bishop Steve and I taught about sixty pastors in Malawi and then in Mozambique, and it was well-received. This teaching is life-changing, and everywhere we go, we hear stories of total transformations in the communities. However, when we arrived in Botswana, they were very negative, saying, "We don't want your teaching, and we don't understand what it is all about."

They agreed to meet, and the next day, we gave them an outline of its transformative results. When finished, they openly said, "We desperately need your program; when are you able to return? The local copper mine closed down recently with the loss of six thousand jobs. People are desperate, with some committing suicide and others returning to their villages." A world-renowned prophet had recently visited and told them that God was sending help and not to be afraid. We agreed to return as soon as possible.

Before we left Botswana, I was asked to speak at a national conference for widows. I told them about the widow's group that had transformed a village. "You also can be agents of change in your community, everyone of you." It was such a challenge for them, for widows are amongst the poorest in the land.

While John Wesley's guidelines had settled an election in the past, it had not been carried into the future. So, I had purposefully left my trip to Kenya until the political polls were over, as from that time on, unrest was usual. However, the Government decided to re-run the elections, so I was in

Kenya at a time of great turmoil. There were demonstrations in Nairobi, and the police tear-gassed those in the crowd who were fighting, looting, and overturning cars. I knew that God was my protection. An Australian woman was shot dead, and my family was convinced it was me and they needed great reassurance.

In Nairobi, I had a long discussion with Situma about the unrest. He told me that the churches were trying to get the opposing parties together to talk and that he had been appointed as the primary resource for them. How greatly I admired this quiet, unassuming man. How grateful I was to God for bringing us together, for he has had such an influence on the development of Commutrem.

It had long ago been agreed that within five years Commutrem would become self-sufficient. I travelled to Kitale on 19 September to discuss how the handover would occur. A few days later, I caught a forty-seater plane back to Nairobi, and in flying high above the Rift Valley, I saw hundreds of thousands of flamingo in Lake Nakuru; it was a stunning sight. The trip continued on over to Mount Longonot- inside a volcano was a beautiful green lake. I will always remember this fantastic, unforgettable experience.

Back in Nairobi, my friend Maxine joined me for those last few weeks and taught the discipleship course with me. Three days before we were due to fly back to Australia, disaster struck. I was in Archbishop Simon's house in Nairobi. For some time, the rain had been relentlessly pelting down, and some of it leaked through the roof, forming a puddle on the floor. One morning I woke to water everywhere, and I slipped, fell and hit my head. Maxine thought I had been completely knocked out, and rightly so, for I was unconscious.

For the next eight hours, I was completely unaware of being taken to three different hospitals, and in the long term, I never did regain the memory of that day. The first local hospital sent me for a scan at a larger hospital. That hospital couldn't get the results quickly, and this was a problem as we were due to fly back to Australia two days later. So I was sent on further. At the final hospital, the scan was completed. Within a few hours, the results showed a bleed to the brain, now subsiding. The nurses and doctors said, 'she must have a very good God because this should be much more serious than it is.' When I became conscious, I was surrounded by seven people, including the bishops and their wives and Maxine. They told me that I had been very flirtatious, and the mind boggles at what I might have said to those standing by listening to me.

Within a couple of days, I was discharged and promptly changed my flight details to fly with Maxine as I did not want to do the return trip alone, having recently had a brain bleed. I was so grateful to have Maxine looking after me. She certainly a God-send. Without her loving care, I could not have survived.

2018

Back home, I continued refining both of the programs that I was teaching in Africa. A committee member showed me how to compile the teaching in a "train the trainer" format. At the time, I was still having trouble believing God for finances. Commonly, to allay my fears and somewhat increase my faith, I had a particular financial blessing come my way. Margot rang from England with the glad news that Edith, a beautiful 94-year-old Christian lady, had come into an inheritance and wanted to give $5,000 to the work in Zimbabwe. Praise God! The money was a confirmation that I did not need to worry.

The story doesn't stop there. Edith has a friend Kate who for many years worked as a doctor. After her recent retirement, she promptly volunteered to work at an Anglican Bible college in Zimbabwe. She learned of the community development work and asked if we would consider training their bible students and teach them about developing their community. The following year we trained seventy of those students. I must admit that now we had training units in seven different countries, costing $50,000 annually to support; I was having trouble believing that God could supply that much money. He reassured me time and time again with verses from the bible and even open visions, but it was a battle for me. A favourite saying of Hudson Taylor was, "God's work, done in God's way, will never lack God's supply." But it was easier to believe this with my head than it was to embrace it with my heart.

32

NETWORKING

Bishop Simon and Bishop Martin had received invitations to attend the inaugural Elim Global Leaders' conference - the first of its kind. The conference was to be held at the headquarters in Malvern in England. There in their grounds were memorials for ten of their missionaries who were martyred in Eldoret, Kenya - only an hour's drive from where much of our initial work with Commutrem began.

Elim is a Pentecostal movement born out of the Welsh revival and travels very close to the heart of God. Bishop Martin approached the organisers with the idea of bringing me along with them, but I was given a complete refusal, even though I had been working closely with the Elim church. "She is not a member of any Elim church - very few exist in Australia," they retorted. Bishop Simon then said, "Well, if she isn't coming, we are not coming either. Marie is part of our team." So, they relented, and I came along too. Bishop Simon, the only overseas delegate invited to speak, spoke on business and the gospel. I was told he was invited to speak because of his involvement with the Community Development Program.

Bishops from many developing countries were keen to know more, so it was an excellent opportunity to network. As we interacted with the delegates from fifty different countries, I could see the hand of God preparing the way to fulfil the vision to end world poverty throughout the developing countries. After the conference, the bishops and I visited Margot, and she put on a buffet and invited all her friends. About twenty people came, all of whom were interested in the work in Africa. From this small gathering, a committee in England was set up. God was continually opening doors, and I was beginning to understand that this was His work, and as such, He was at the helm leading the way.

A few days later, I enjoyed a train ride up to London for a day of sightseeing. I love London and always have found its history, at every turn, fascinating. On my return journey, I discovered that my purse, with all of my cards and $300, had been stolen. This was a big blow as I was leaving for Kenya within a few days. I promptly cancelled all the cards and was reassured by the bank that a replacement credit card would be sent out immediately. It was a comedy of errors with many promises never kept. I was in Africa for three months, and I never received a replacement card but used the travel card I had kept separately.

Maxine joined me shortly after I arrived in Kenya, and we spent a lot of the three weeks she was with me praying for the work. On one of those days, God reminded me "to spend and be spent in the Masters' service." He went on to say that the fields are white and ready to be harvested, and I was to pray that the Master would send labourers into the fields. I knew it was time to get more serious about employing coordinators for Uganda, Tanzania, Zimbabwe, Zambia, Malawi, Mozambique, and Kenya and training them up.

Maxine also helped me with the discipleship training program so those converted through the community development program would have a firm foundation for their faith.

Bishop John did much of that teaching, and many people received the baptism of the Holy Spirit, and it was like a mini-revival. God told me that I was in a training school of ministry, learning how to lay hands on people, minister to them, and speak out in prophecy. Maxine also taught some of the teachings with me and even preached several times. She always returned to Australia feeling refreshed and energised.

I was teaching the community development program alongside Bishop Steve. From Nairobi, we then planned to travel to Mombasa by train as the car journey was very long. I was packed and ready to leave at 10.00 am, but Bishop Steve did not arrive until 1.30 pm. Knowing about African time, I was not concerned and thought he would know how long it took to reach the train station. Unfortunately, we were caught in a traffic jam, so Bishop Steve said, "Right, we will catch a piki-piki. The two of us jumped out of the Uber and hopped onto a piki-piki. He then cut across all the lanes of speeding traffic and sped down a steep incline onto the station. I was terrified. We arrived just as the train was disappearing into the distance. We had missed it! As we were scheduled to teach the following morning, we hastily caught a plane, which cost $800. I was not amused and resented paying that money out.

A few days later, I travelled onwards to Kitale for the Annual National Conference for the Kenyan Elim church. Bishop Simon, who had started the Elim church in Kenya, gave a compelling opening address to about six hundred people.

God gave me a word for this group, and He said, He would "ignite an eternal fire in our hearts, one that would never be quenched. It was a new day, and the fire was to go far and wide, and many dry and barren hearts would be set alight with God's love."

During that conference, I met up with a bishop. He is a great man of faith and had worked in some of the semi-desert areas. He told me a story about when he lived in Turkana, where most people still live a traditional lifestyle and wear traditional clothing. He had worked in refugee camps for many years. This Bishop told me a fantastic story of a Muslim who had become a Christian and returned to his own country. There, his family disowned him. They said he was no longer married because he had converted, and his children were no longer his. He decided to move to another country. But they found where he was, captured him, took him into the desert, tied him to a tree, and said, "recant, and we will free you," but he refused. So, they left him in fifty-degree heat and told him they would return in twenty-four hours to kill him if he did not recant. When they returned, he said, "I will never recant. Jesus is my Lord." At this, a man took a gigantic sword and was about to decapitate him when a snake came out of a bush and fastened to his hand. The men, in shock ,ran away. A couple of hours later, a shepherd boy found this courageous believer. He ran to his village, and they came and set him free. It's a stern rebuke to most of us in the west. This Bishop remarkably preached the next day on "the glorious church," the pattern in the book of Acts. In Africa, the level of faith is so high that it is like living in the New Testament times. He is a living example of this.

It was at this particular conference Bishop Simon was consecrated as Archbishop of Kenya. It was a very moving ceremony, and he had all of the regalia that the Archbishop of Canterbury wears. On the final day of the conference, there was great rejoicing as about one hundred students were ordained as pastors, associate pastors, and graduands from the Haapnet Bible College. Alongside some of the delegates, I was asked to pray with and prophesy over those being ordained.

While at the conference, Situma and I managed some time alone to talk over various problems within the program. Concerning the scarcity of water in the Voi area, he told me that he had just finished designing a free course on environmental farming for Thika, Nairobi university. Again, I marvelled at how God had provided such an amazing servant of His to help us fulfill our vision in Africa.

Back in Nairobi, a newly ordained pastor had just been appointed to start a church in a local slum area. He felt out of his depth as there were so many under the influence of drugs and alcohol, and he did not know where to begin. This young pastor had been brought up in a slum and had been 'a naughty boy' (his words) until he met Jesus. In facing a daunting future with enormous tasks ahead of him, he asked me to teach him the community development course. I agreed to teach him privately as I had a couple of days spare. He and his beautiful wife had such loving hearts for the poor. How could I refuse?

During a Sunday morning service, a visiting prophet prophesied over this young pastor. He saw him working with marginalised poverty-stricken people in a slum area using an outreach program. The program was everything I had taught him just a few days before. This prophetic word was such an encourouragment as he began the enormous task of ministering in such difficult areas.

33

THE LEADING

My only travel card had run out by this time, and I was frustrated and not impressed with my bank, even though it is one of the biggest in Australia - for I had to contact Margot and ask her to send me some money.

Bishop John, Bishop Martin, and Bishop Steve drove me to Tanzania for the Elim National Conference a few days later. On the 15-hour trip, the road was lonely, and as we drove across the border into Tanzania, some men, covered in extra thick black pigment, jumped out and threw something in front of our car and then raced back into the bush. The men probably had in mind to puncture the tyres so they could rob us. Bishop John swerved to avoid the obstacle, and we sped on.

The conference atmosphere was very political. The attending pastors and bishops said they did not want any preaching but only wanted to vote for church positions. Archbishop Simon was their guest speaker, and he spoke with great courage and told them God was not pleased with their attitudes. He spoke about the birth of a baby – the stages it went through and challenged the Tanzanian church to give back the church to its mother and allow the Holy Spirit to nurture and care for it once again.

I also had a prophetic word. I felt God was saying that our hearts were cluttered, and Jesus wanted to clean them out and place an eternal flame there. Bishop Martin also had a picture of a heart like a fist, unable to receive. There was a coldness and barrenness in many at the conference. On the final day of the conference, the Lord gave me another message.

"You think you have come here to vote, but I have brought you here to hear my word. You are my appointed under-

shepherds, and your flock is starving. You are to go home and feed them the word that I will give you here at the conference." The pastors heard this, reassessed their priorities, and the atmosphere changed dramatically.

One night at the conference, I was in unbearable pain. It was a longstanding problem, but this night it had never been so bad. My mattress was rock solid, and it being hard as nails were exacerbating the problem. The pain was so bad that I was biting my fingers until 3 am that morning to prevent my crying out. "*If only I had a doona, I could place it under me to make the mattress softer.*" But where was I to get such a thing in the middle of Africa? The next day a travelling salesman came to the hotel. Usually, they just sell little knick- knacks, but I saw doonas strapped to his back as he was leaving. I raced after him and bought one. Sure enough, that night, I slept soundly. How like our Lord to provide for me in this way. I had never before seen anyone selling doonas in Africa. Most likely an angel. To me, it was a miracle.

I was invited to the official opening of a new church that Bishop John had planted back in Nairobi. It was held in a big tent in a field. I became aware of a colossal figure seated on a mound of earth outside the tent as I sat there. In this vision, I heard it say, "this is my territory. I have reigned here for hundreds of years sitting on this throne. There is no way I am moving," he said belligerently. I was nonplussed - *what should I do with this vision*? I thought, so I consulted Bishop Martin, he said," you have been shown this, so we will know how to pray."

As we started praying, a bright light began to permeate the tent, and the figure outside began to shrink. The last I saw of him, he was scurrying away to get out of the light. A few days later, I visited the tent, and I saw the light penetrating the farthest corners of the field and from the dark recesses tumbled snakes, scorpions, and spiders- all desperate to escape the light. The kingdom of light had overcome the kingdom of darkness.

***

It is said that God leads His children step by step. It is only as I look back that I have been aware of such leading throughout my life. Back in Australia, springtime was bursting with new life, and I was invited to stay in Bundeena for a month to keep my daughter-in-law's mother company while she and my son travelled overseas. I love the beautiful setting in the Royal National Park, and I gladly obliged to stay.

Every Sunday while there, I went to the local church. It was held in a cottage and simply had a beautiful feel to it. Perhaps it was the salt air or its quaint size. Whatever it was, I simply loved attending this church. Afterward, there was always lunch on the balcony, so I stayed back and sat next to a lady and began chatting to her. She told me that she had just returned from a mission trip to Africa and had been over there with the primary purpose of supporting the poor in small villages. The person who organised the trip was a pastor of the Church of Christ, and he had been doing it for over twenty years and was very experienced. I made an appointment to see him, and over coffee, he came to hear what we were doing with the community development and practical skills program.

We arranged for him to come to our next committee meeting to discuss how we might work together. We realised that there were synergies in what we were doing. He also agreed to travel to Kenya to see our work there. Just through a simple conversation over lunch, another door miraculously opened.

In December, it was my eightieth birthday. My family celebrated the occasion with a lavish afternoon tea at Sydney's famous Intercontinental Hotel. It was a beautifully posh afternoon, and it sure was wonderful to be surrounded by my sons and their families. Then, with my friends I had an open day- and Angela and Robyn organised everything.

Visitors, as early as 11 am, came to celebrate with me.

As we all sat around, I told everyone of my gratitude to God, for he had rescued me in my early twenties when a life of partying caused me to suffer much emptiness. Life was not worth living, and I was contemplating suicide. I told how God worked in my life over the past eighty years and shared some of the amazing answers to prayer throughout my walk with Him. The last of my visitors left just after three o'çlock, and, looking out over my lounge room, I could still hear the happy sound of singing, praying, and laughter. I could hear a softer sound of cups clanking and the "thanks so much" as delicious cakes were being served and, even softer still, of serviettes, scrumpled on chairs and crumbs all over the table. These two celebrations were a perfect end to another very eventful year.

34

THE HIGH TEA

I started the New Year at a four-day conference on discovering your spiritual gifts with my friend Jane. It was very inspiring, especially the afternoon I went with another to a local shopping mall. There I was to develop my gift of evangelism in an environment that isn't all that friendly towards spiritual things. We offered to pray with anyone who felt they had a need. Everyone, including those experiencing grief, injustice, financial needs, and employment opportunities all were appreciative of our prayers. There are so many needs out there in the community, and so often, we sit in our churches' safety and never go out and minister to them.

When the pastor taught on the gifts of the Holy Spirit, he had a vision. He was walking on a wide road littered with armour that Christians had thrown onto the side of the road. God said that I was still wearing my armour, but it wasn't ready for battle. The sword was rusty, and the direction I took needed more peace within it; I needed more faith to protect me in life, and I needed to see myself as God's righteous child more than I did. This essentially is what he meant when He said the shield of faith and breastplate of righteousness. They both need us to become more aware of them, and this was quite a challenge.

Now that we had a training unit with Haapnet in seven different countries, the cost of financing this had escalated to $50,000 a year. So, we decided to set up a fund-raising committee. The first event was a high tea. There was a lot of hard work put into this, and the afternoon high tea was magnificent. Homemade sandwiches, cakes, mini quiches and scones, and savories were all served on Royal Doulton china. I spoke about the program, and we invited people to help support it financially. It raised about $1,000. One of the ladies recorded my talk on her phone, and she sent it to her son in Chicago. This young man was very impressed that the program helped pastors and leaders mobilise their communities in setting up small businesses. He was tremendously excited as our program meshed nicely with his desire to teach business principles in Africa. He was in the process of relocating back to Australia and arranged to contact me when he was settled. He also told me that he was financially able to help our projects further.

Even so, within my heart, I still had a lot of misgivings about the availability of finance, and the battle between human reasoning and divine interventions was real. Of course, God knew what was going on with me. Just before the High Tea, He gave me a vision of a vast treasure chest full of finances for the project. Then I was shown Him upturning it and me catching hundreds of gold coins as they cascaded into my leather apron. I knew God could provide, but my question was, would He.

I felt way too insignificant that He would visit me with His favour, and I even could not figure out why He would bless me in such an extraordinary way. But even so, there was a very persistent person in me, one who would, against the odds, never give up. I held on to every bit of faith that I had, and as a result, the days shortly after the vision were full of dramatic events.

I was throwing out some old papers, and on top of the pile, I noticed a cheque for $360. It was fifteen years old, but the company said they would place the money into my account within seventy-two hours. Then my insurance company rang me to say that the boundary where I lived had changed, and they were going to reimburse me $150 as I was now living in a safer locality. I found some old foreign currency that was worth $150 when exchanged. Finally, someone I barely know handed me a $100 note for Africa. God was showing me that my fears were unfounded and that he would provide.

The members of the Australian Committee were working very hard. The new treasurer soon had organised for us to become a charity with tax exemptions. This incorporation was a significant step, for without it we could not apply for funding.

On a personal note, I was still suffering intense pain and had been referred to a specialist. There was a long waiting time of three months, but after prayer, I was given an appointment the very next day due to a cancellation. She diagnosed the problem as nerve pain and prescribed some tablets. I was sternly warned never to attend either a chiropractor, a physiotherapist, or go to the gym. On my way to Kenya via England, I completely forgot what she said and took myself off to an osteopath for back pain. When I arrived at London airport to catch the plane to Kenya, I was in agony. I could not sit, stand, or walk, and was taken to the plane in a wheelchair.

As the air hostess organised the luggage in lockers above, I squirmed to find a comfortable position when suddenly I was pain-free. The pain disappeared, and the soft seat was enough to ease it, and I did not have any trouble throughout the entire flight.

Six months later, at a check-up, the specialist said, "This is a miracle, for a woman of your age does not respond in this way." I praised God, and she replied, "yes, you can praise the good Lord, for He has done it."

I arrived in Nairobi at the end of May, and Maxine had flown in to join me for the next three weeks. With her by my side, we spent many long hours in prayer for the program. We taught the discipleship program together at a variety of places. However, the trip to Kenya was not well organised. Typical of their sense of time, often, we would be waiting four or five hours for someone to pick us up. The lack of communication meant that, at times, we were unaware of what was going on. Often various training was cancelled, and we would be waiting for hours; the trip to West Africa was cancelled. Impatience is one of my weaker points, and God was testing me in this area, and I did not always pass the test.

We continued to teach the community development training throughout Kenya, Uganda, and Tanzania. I had previously found the fifteen-hour trip to Tanzania by car strenuous, so I travelled to Mombasa from Nairobi by train. The views through the Tsavo National Park were breathtaking as many wild animals could be seen. I enjoyed this trip immensely and made lots of Kenyan friends. I taught them how to play travel games I learnt in my childhood. They loved it. There was much fun and laughter throughout the journey.

Haapnet hosted a visit from Pastor Paul from the Church of Christ in Sydney. He and his group of eight people wanted to see what we were doing in Africa. We took them to visit various successful projects. Their reaction was unexpected. "Why are you taking us to see these rich people?" They queried. "We want to see those in need." They obviously had not understood that the successful people in the flourishing projects had once been in deep poverty before they had been taught how to set up their small businesses.

35

DROUGHTS AND FIRES

Bishop Martin and I could see the program multiplying at a fast rate. Over many meetings, we were discussing many matters, and it became even more apparent that our policies and procedures needed to be in place, and often, this was a challenge. Situma had done these policies for Commutrem, and he was going to do the same for Haapnet. Then I got some shocking news. His daughter contacted me to tell me that her father had been killed in a car accident. I was devastated. I had such high regard for Situma, as I appreciated his quiet, unassuming manner. He also was highly gifted and had helped us tremendously over the years and rarely was paid for the work he had done. I knew I would miss him greatly and grieved at his loss.

Emmanuel is our skills coordinator. His wife took ill shortly afterward, and due to lack of funds, Naomi was taken by ambulance on a four-hour journey from Nairobi to Eldoret to a less expensive hospital. Any form of sickness can have devastating results, even more so a significant illness, as hospital treatment is expensive, and most cannot afford it.

Bishop Emmanuel became very ill himself, and within a couple of months, he had died. Since we first started, we had made considerable strides in extending the teaching to seven countries and had taught about twenty thousand Africans. We knew our progress would threaten the spirit of poverty which had a stronghold. Voi is probably one of the main areas we have worked in Kenya. Within weeks Bishop David's wife from Voi took sick, and within hours she died. We began to feel that strong spiritual forces were targeting us. I needed a break. I needed to wait more on the Lord.

I had always wanted to go to India and visit Rajasthan. Many years ago, Doug and I planned to visit, but it seemed India would be destined to be struck off our bucket list with a succession of disruptions. After the disaster of 9/11, India and Pakistan were threatening nuclear war, so we postponed it. Shortly afterward, Doug took ill. Then the door opened.

I needed a break, and the opportunity to go to India was now mine. My friend and I stayed in five-star hotels. We hired a car and had a private driver and a guide at each destination. We swam in infinity pools, stayed in Maharajah's palaces and castles, and danced to traditional Indian music. The bazaars were fascinating, and we were intrigued by a decaying town on the Silk Route- which had fallen on hard times. Most of the Havelis (houses) of the wealthy merchants were deserted, crumbling, and decaying. A group of artisans wanted to restore these old houses, and to help them, they set up a creative/art business. Miniature paintings were intricately created using a brush with one hair (I have one hanging on my wall), and hand-embroidered silk articles were sold.

We visited the Boruptor bird sanctuary, a world heritage site, where 2,000,000 migratory birds visit every year. There we enjoyed a ride in a rickshaw to a water hole and then saw seventeen different species of birds, including a spotted owlet and a very rare rose-ringed parakeet. My love for birds made this one of the highlights of the trip. We rode on elephants and camels. Another highlight was a visit to the world-famous Taj Mahal. It took Shah Jahan twenty-two years to build this memorial to his wife, and its beauty was indescribable. Truly a holiday to remember.

December 16 will always be a sacred day for me. As the year drew to a close, I made my annual pilgrimage to Woniora Cemetery. There were lots of tears that day as I viewed the Memorial book and left a rose on its page. Seventeen years after losing Doug, I could still feel the grief and sadness, and I miss him dearly. But that day, too, I thought of the joy that God would allow me to be part of his work in Africa in bringing many people out of poverty, what a great privilege, and I vowed that I would continue as long as I was fit and able to do so.

As I was driving home, I noticed flashing lights behind me. I glanced again in my rear-view mirror and saw that a police car was closely following me. *Well, I'm not speeding, and I am not speaking on my mobile phone, so he must be after someone else,* I thought to myself. Moments later, I heard the siren and realised, *Oh, no, what have I done!!* I quickly pulled over.

"I want to breath-test you," he tersely said.

"Is this your car? Why are you driving so far from home?"

He obviously thought I was on a restricted licence that prevents older people from driving more than 10km from their homes.

"You are in an unregistered vehicle," he remonstrated with me. "You cannot drive anywhere now," he said.

I could not believe it! I was miles from home and on the slip road to a freeway. I was in a real pickle. I held my breath and prayed.

"Look," he said, "you are allowed to drive to a garage and get it registered. It's a $670 fine, but I will let you off this time, but you must go straight to the garage." I was thankful that he had relented in charging me.

***

The year ended with a national drought, severe water restrictions, and horrific bush fires. The fires raged through hundreds of towns on the entire east coast and even reached South Australia and Kangaroo Island. Some of the raging fires were close by, and many from our church in Picton were evacuated and badly affected. One lady was evacuated three times when the fire got within one street of her home. Her family prayed, and the wind miraculously changed directions, and her home was saved. The fires raged up and down the coastline, and what seemed over a month, ash and charred leaves were floating in the atmosphere. We were constantly surrounded by thick smoke, and the air quality dangerously fell way below average. Many with breathing problems were seriously affected.

The fires continue to rage throughout New South Wales reaching a crisis point. But if we thought the situation close to our home was devastating, the situation on the south coast was much worse. The navy was brought in to evacuate people forced onto beaches, and the army was seconded to help fight the fires.

Then, if that wasn't enough, March 2020 had another major shock in store. It was reported that a mysterious illness was sweeping the world – the COVID 19 pandemic had begun. Little were we to know that it would travel from country to country, bringing death and destruction in its wake. Millions of people in America and the United Kingdom were hospitalized, and many of them died including some medical staff.

In Australia, due to the very swift action of the government led by our Christian prime minister, Scott Morrison, the result was much less lethal. At its peak, seven hundred people a day were being diagnosed with COVID19. Churches were closed intermittently throughout the year, and services went online, which I found technically challenging.

Lockdowns became the norm. I spent more and more time in prayer. God had told me many years ago that I could pray small prayers or big prayers. The choice was mine, but He is a big God. I was led more and more to pray big prayers as I waited in the solitude- confined to home.

So now I look back over the years

And I have seen myself catching His tears.
Helping the lost in a land far away
On a path winding upwards
My heart, it would stay.
Now smitten by love and held fast by hope,
the poor entwined within
His loving Hand and mine.

Upward Path © Jenny Marsland 2020

36

UNSTOPPABLE

At the epidemic's beginning, it was believed throughout the world that a vaccine could not possibly be produced before the middle of 2021. However, I felt God tell me that it would be available by the end of the year. And so it was, as scientists throughout the world worked tirelessly for a breakthrough. The federal government brought the state and federal leaders together for a national cabinet, and with excellent cooperation, they tackled the vast problem together.

Huge queues began forming outside Centrelink as millions were put out of work. I was deeply concerned about all those out of work, especially the overseas students, as they could not return home due to travel restrictions. The hospitality industry had been severely affected, and most had lost their jobs. After speaking with our pastor's wife, we agreed to set up a food hamper service for them, supplying a fortnightly box of fresh fruit and vegetables and staples.

This was soon extended to the residents of Spring Farm, where our church is situated. As we took one step forward, God began to open doors. Ralf, from Microlend, offered us money to buy items and space to pack and store the food. Very soon, we outgrew this space, and Daniel, a member of our church, offered us space in his warehouse. He and the church supplied financial assistance for staples and fresh fruit and vegetables. We soon had a small group of volunteers working on this with us.

As we reached out in love into our community, God spoke to me at this time and told me He had spent the whole of my life preparing me for the task He had given me in Africa. So, while I couldn't visit Africa due to COVID, the vision to end poverty in the developing world never wavered. God had given us this vision, and He would bring it to pass. In the meantime, throughout this challenging time, the work continued through weekly conversations with Bishop Martin.

Then in a text, I received this message from Bishop Martin. He said, "In my devotion this morning, God placed my heart's attention on the message you sent. "We will run the race set before us and not be distracted from our end goal to eradicate world poverty." He continued, "the more I pray with these words, the more the Lord affirms in my spirit that if we refuse to be distracted, maintain a walk of faith and focus on Christ the author and finisher of this vision, we will see the Lord move across the world raising the lowly and the poor from the dungeon of oppression and afflictions...

We will be Christ's feet (walking in the streets and lives of the outcasts in society) and Christ's hands (embracing the most hurting with love). Then shall the light of the Lord shine among the nations, and the good news of the kingdom of God be proclaimed higher and further in the earth...

Be encouraged, Marie, you are championing a global vision that God is turning to be His banner and safety net for the weak, which is the cry of all the bible prophets and the Law of Moses. I just found it such a privilege to work alongside such a servant of God! Thanks Marie, for carrying the heart of God."

It was impossible to travel to Africa, so it was decided to spend the time compiling our policies and procedures here in Australia. I worked with Jill, a solicitor. We had already become a charity with tax deductibility status thanks to our treasurer, Shireen. God was positioning us for our next stage of growth, and we needed to be ready.

The work continued apace in Africa, despite COVID. The new coordinators in the seven East African countries were well established and were very eager to reach out into their hurting communities. Bishop Martin was zooming sessions teaching them the Community Development program. They were so excited, and even before they had finished, some had begun taking the training into their communities.

Ps Rose, who worked for the Elim church, became a country coordinator, and began teaching the women's groups in Zimbabwe. She gushed, "Thank you, our bishops Martin and Steve, for the wonderful work in empowering the African continent. You are highly favoured to be workers in God's vineyard."

Bishop Raphael began to gather interdenominational groups in Tanzania for training. He said, "This is a new beginning for Tanzania and Africa. I can't wait to get into the community and tell them about this good news."

In Kenya, Rev Lazarus began to teach many groups, commenting to Bishop Martin, "Thanks to all those who have cared enough to see poverty and human degradation fixed and the restoration of human dignity. The Lord has made you the agents of our transformation, and when all is done, you will not miss God's blessings now and in the age to come."

They could not contain their enthusiasm. The training provided great possibilities and they all could see how it was revolutionising their communities.

Bishop Martin could not wait to share with me these comments. "It is so humbling," he said, "to see enthusiastic fellow Africans eager to give a 'hand up' to other Africans. It was so exciting. To see how our God had touched the hearts of His servants and filled them with the desire to see their fellow Africans brought out of poverty and into tremendous freedom. For sure, the poor have a place to play in walking themselves out of their social, economic, spiritual, intellectual, and physical poverty."

One night at 3 am, when in prayer, he received a vision. In it, he saw devastation. "There was massive flooding, hunger, hopelessness, and women were running for help with their children on their backs and holding others by their hands. They were without help. I then saw giant fig trees blossoming and bearing massive fruit. The trees were so big that the branches were interlocked, and I was moving from one fig tree to another through the interlocking branches, harvesting the figs, which were big, sweet, and good-looking. I didn't understand the meaning of the vision and therefore started praying and looking for the meaning of the fig tree in the bible...

I have understood now that in biblical times, the fig tree represented the nations. The fig tree has two seasons – spring in April when the tree produces small and not very sweet fruit referred to as "poor man's food"- this is the similar season when Jesus passed it and cursed it for lack of fruit. The second is autumn/October and November when it bears massive/big and sweet fruit referred to as the "rich man's food."

He said that the Lord "revealed that He had opened a door into the nations we are seeking to reach." Bishop Martin went on to say, "I am praying that as we trust God, He will cause us to witness this abundant harvest among the countries in Africa and the world. That through the community development program, we will experience massive fruition. Bitterness, pain, poverty, human dignity, degradation, and hopelessness will be replaced by a season of a great harvest of joy. I vowed that I would continue the work He has entrusted to me to its very end as long as I am able...

I pray that God will enable me to serve Him and minister to those in need. Not only to show the way out of poverty but also to show the way into eternal life. The abundant life He promises in His word is God's exceeding grace of salvation and service to Him by people from all tongues, race, and nations."

"Lord," He said, "bring in the harvest in our days. Use us, use our partners, the country coordinators, and coming new networks to bring in community transformation and a great harvest for your kingdom. May the Lord feed the hungry with the abundance of figs- the "rich man's food."

What a challenge yet such a privilege to work with someone who walks so close to God.

Towards the end of the year, an American pastor visited Kenya and spoke with Bishop Martin about extending our discipleship program - the one I had been running since I first went to Africa. Their more intensive training took our discipleship program to another level. To extend what we were already doing was a logic move and I saw this offer as a fantastic opportunity. We welcomed it with open arms.

2020 was finished by God showing me that discipleship and ministering to the poor were the two threads going through my life and that He would support and ensure both would succeed.

37

GOD'S GLORY

At the beginning of 2021, again we were caught unawares as the Delta variant of COVID swept through New South Wales and Victoria. At the height of the pandamic, the numbers contracting the disease mounted to over two thousand per day. As more and more people became vaccinated reaching over 80% with double vaccination, the pandamic began to subside.

As the pandamic began easing, God impressed upon my mind the word EXPLOSION! I was unsure what this meant. Then, during one of my daily walks around the neighbourhood, He pointed out a stand of trees. They looked absolutely dead. I remember seeing them last winter and thinking *they will never come to life. They are totally dead.* How wrong I was. I saw those trees again in spring, and they had exploded into new growth. They were utterly alive. God showed me that this is what will happen with the Community Development program, the Discipleship Program, and the finances. A couple of days after receiving this word, we saw an explosion in the finances and received a $25,000 donation. Praise God.

As we have stepped out in faith in the seven countries, this donation will help us run the program in every one of those countries.

We are now trusting God to provide for the other thirteen countries. They are keenly waiting for us to develop the Community Development training for them so that they too may see poverty put to flight. The discipleship program has also exploded into the seven countries. In Kenya, Bishop Martin has trained eighteen regional bishops. They will each, in turn, teach all the pastors in their regions, who will then teach those in their congregations. Meanwhile in Africa the discipleship program was sweeping through Kenya. As regional bishops passed the teaching to local pastors and then onto their congregations. "The impact is enornmous," enthused Bishop Martin. No longer will Christianity in Kenya be described as "one thousand kilometres wide and one centimetre deep." They are building their faith on the solid rock!

I vowed that as long as I am able

I will continue to its very end the work He has

entrusted to me.

I pray God will enable me to serve Him and minister to

those in need,

not only the way out of poverty but the way into eternal
life,

the abundant life He promises.

What an amazing God we have.

REFERENCES

Grumond, 2021. Edelweiss Flower meaning, symbolism and Uses- Petal Republic http://www.petalrepublic.com/edelweiss-flower)

Taylor, H 1998 Hudson Taylor and the China Inland Mission *The Growth of a Work of God* OMF International. 2 Cluny Road, Singapore 259570

Tomkins, S 2003 *John Wesley A Biography.* William B. Eerdmans Publishing Company. Grand Rapids MI United States of America

Williamson, J E 2011 *Going Forward on Your Knees A New Biography,* Milton Keynes, MKI 9GG

If you feel you'd like to support
our God-given task
of ending world poverty,
please contact
us at www.cdprojects.org